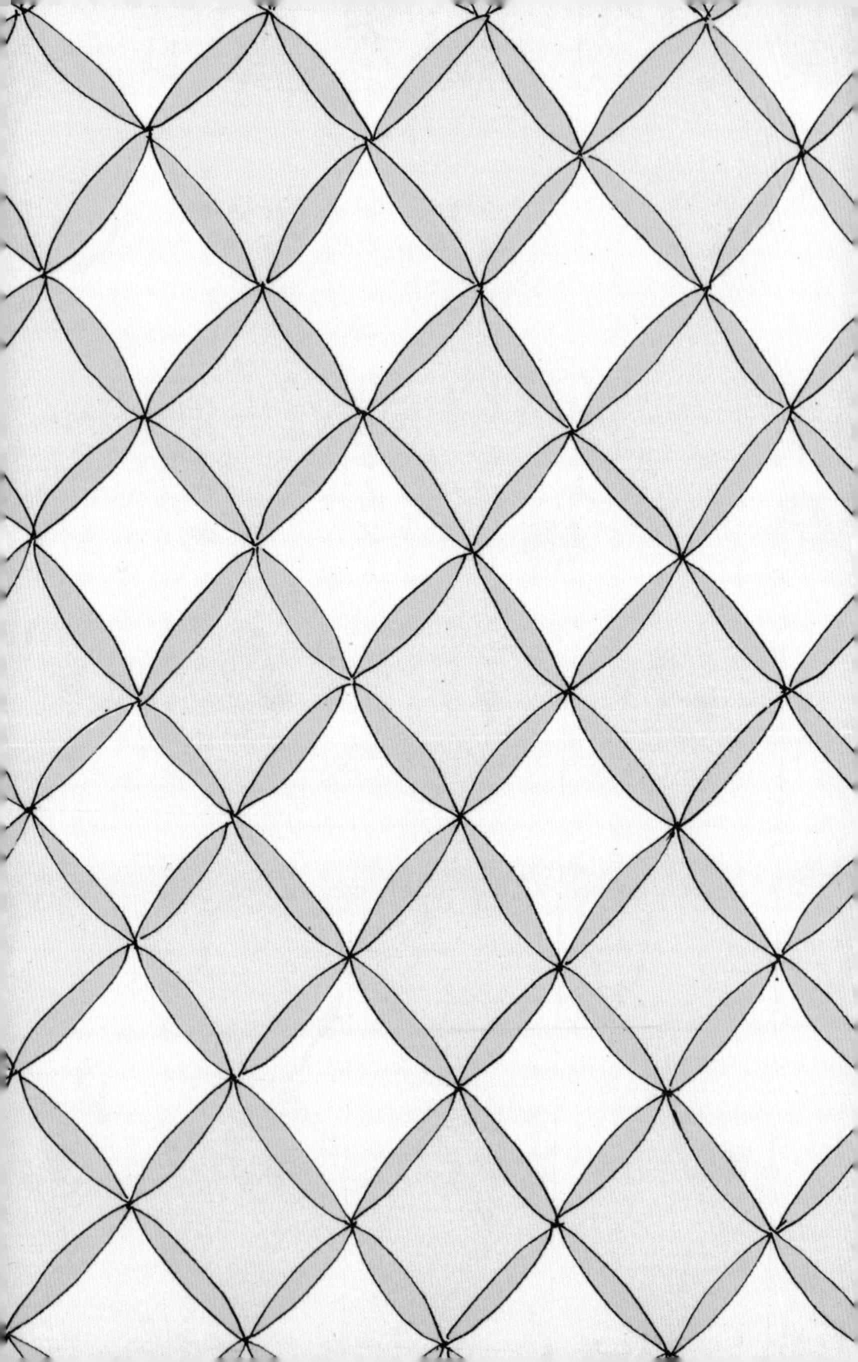

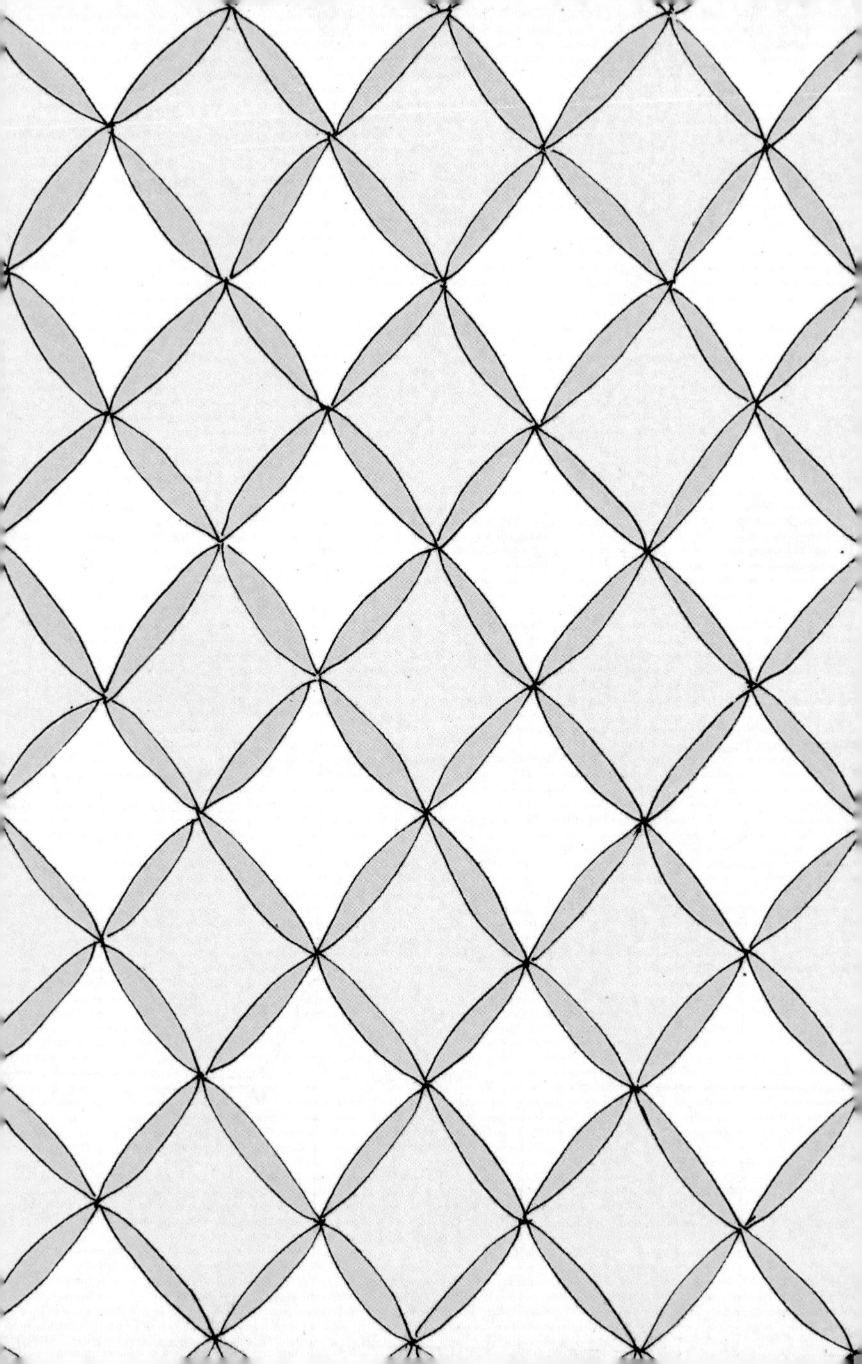

Also by Patricia Marx with Roz Chast

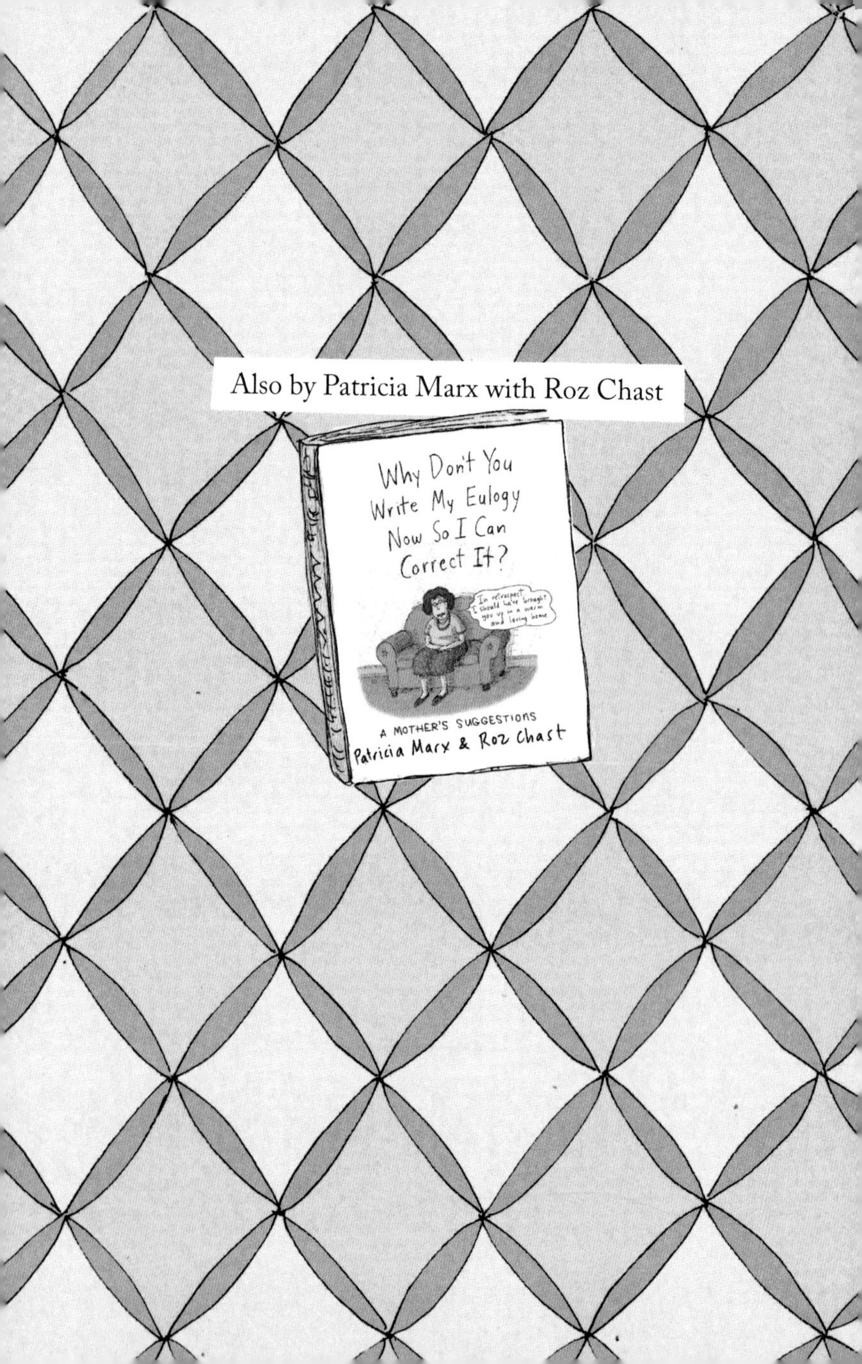
Why Don't You Write My Eulogy Now So I Can Correct It?
In retrospect I should have brought you up in a warm and loving home
A MOTHER'S SUGGESTIONS
Patricia Marx & Roz Chast

YOU CAN ONLY YELL AT ME FOR ONE THING AT A TIME

RULES FOR COUPLES

Patricia Marx

Illustrated by
Roz Chast

CELADON BOOKS, NEW YORK

For information, address Celadon Books, a Division of Macmillan Publishers, 120 Broadway, New York, NY 10271.

www.celadonbooks.com

Endpaper illustrations by Roz Chast

Designed by Jonathan Bennett

ISBN 978-1-250-22513-9 (hardcover)
ISBN 978-1-250-22512-2 (ebook)

Our books may be purchased in bulk for promotional, educational, or business use. Please contact your local bookseller or the Macmillan Corporate and Premium Sales Department at 1-800-221-7945, extension 5442, or by email at MacmillanSpecialMarkets@macmillan.com.

First Edition: January 2020

10 9 8 7 6 5 4 3 2 1

Roz: To all of my significant others in my past, present, and future lives.

Patty: To those, and a few insignificant ones, too.

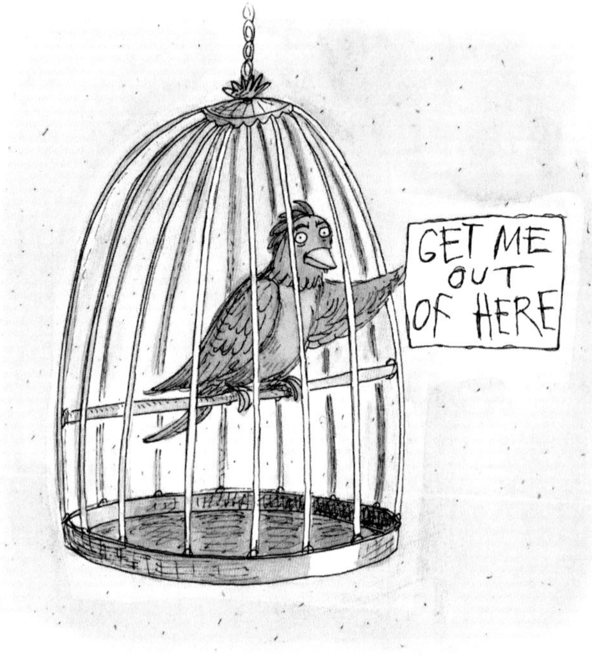
GET ME OUT OF HERE

Introduction

Falling in love is easy. Agreeing about how to load the dishwasher is hard. This is a book of guidelines, tips, and strategies for couples who wish to coexist in happiness. Or at least harmony. Or at least not be worse off than they were before reading these pages.

But advice is for later. This is the introduction, so first a little about Roz and Patty.

Roz has been married to Bill for thirty-five years. They have two children and two birds. The children no longer live at home, but the birds do, and not only because they are in cages.

Patty has lived with Paul for twelve years. Instead of children, they have a robot vacuum cleaner. Patty and Paul were introduced by a mutual friend. "He's perfect," the friend said about Paul. "Perfect is not my type," said Patty.

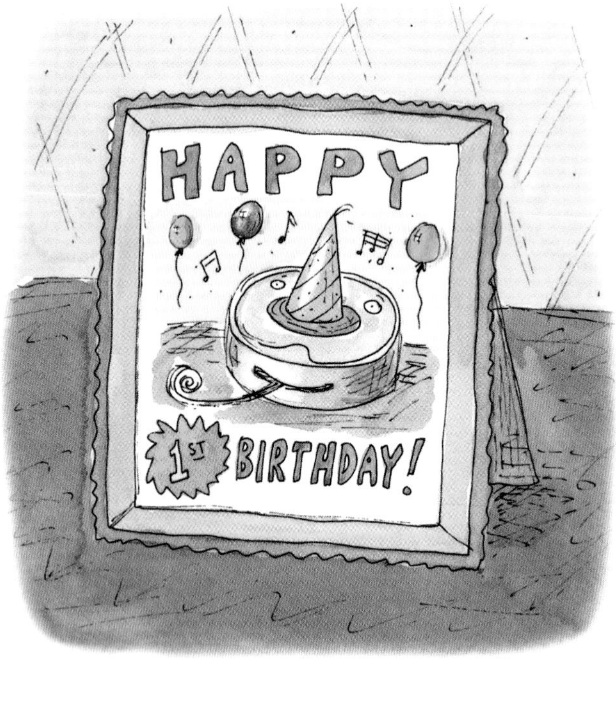
HAPPY
1ST BIRTHDAY!

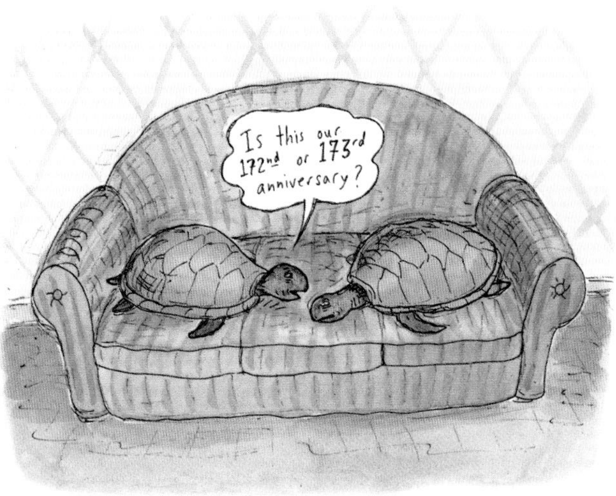
Is this our 172nd or 173rd anniversary?

Neither Patty nor Roz has ever been divorced, though Patty once broke up with someone who had not been aware until then that he'd been dating her.

DR. KIBBLE'S
BATH SERUM
FACIAL SAUCE
EYEBROW CLEANSER
DR. KIBBLE'S
MIRACLE
DR. KIBBLE'S
Eyelid Toner
PROBIOTICS
ORGANIC COMPOUND K
DR. KIBBLE'S
RUTABAGA OINTMENT
DR. KIBBLE'S
LEAVE-IN SCRUB

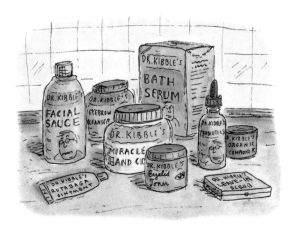

What is it like to be with someone year after year after year after year after year after year after year after year after year after year after year after year after year?

People leave socks on the floor, tell endless stories with irrelevant details, litter the bathroom with so many potions it looks like a meth lab, put the subtitles on during the news even though the show is in perfectly understandable English, invest your joint savings in cryptocurrency, forget to recycle the plastic pouches from FedEx, place dirty dishes near instead of in the sink, will not admit there is a correct way to hang a roll of toilet paper on the holder, insist on making you leave for the airport too early or too late, say *aah* after taking a gulp of water, and make whistling sounds while sleeping.

In an effort to sum up the experience, Patty recalls an incident that happened to her and Paul on a starry summer night many years ago. Strolling along the streets of New York City, they came upon a small park. It was the most picturesque and enchanting scene you can imagine. "Look how the moonlight falls perfectly on the path," said Patty. "Look how that couple sitting on the bench is positioned artistically off center—like in an Impressionist painting," said Paul, adding that the high-rise building in the near background seemed to complete the picture. The two were overcome with the magic of the night. Then a woman they couldn't see screamed, "Action!" A ray of light beamed onto a top floor of the high-rise and a figure appeared. Unknowingly, Patty and Paul had wandered onto the set of *Spider-Man*. If this story were a parable, the lesson would be that life is romantic at first but then the lights go on, and before long, you are both on the subway home, where you might share a pizza or watch a TV show about international terrorism.

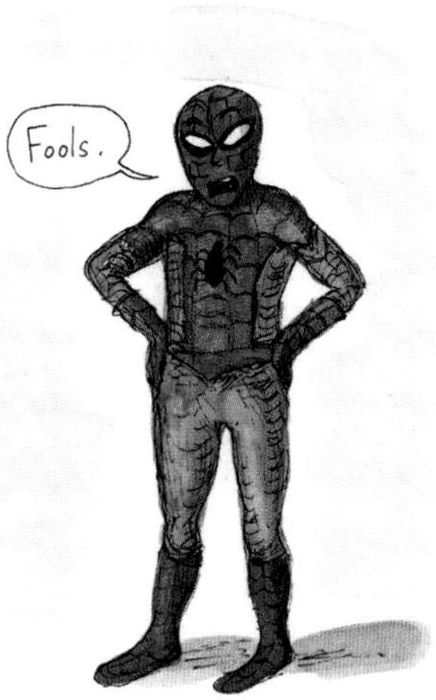
Fools.

Roz has a different metaphor to describe what it's like to make your way through life with someone. Here's how it goes. At birth, you—an ox—are allotted a cart that contains your baggage: your hopes and dreams, but also your phobias, your hang-ups, your obsessions, and whatever mental, physical, and emotional stuff you inherited from your ox parents. Wherever you go, you must lug your cart behind you. But someday you might meet a *special ox*. If you are "serious" about each other, you will be issued a couples cart into which both of you can now throw all your crap. The cart is heavy and a little unwieldy. If you have children, for a stretch you will be lugging them as well. One day, one of you will want to turn down Old Huckleberry Lane because there's a cute little farmers' market down there, and the other will want to stay on I-95. You will have a fight, but eventually work it out because (this is important!): no one gets to steer the cart all the time. On the bright side, if one of you has a sore ankle, the other can work a little harder to pull the cart, and vice versa. Besides, it's more fun to have another ox with whom to pull the goddamn cart. You can gossip about other oxen and discuss various ox-centric topics, and if you are lucky, you can make each other laugh. "Look, there's Farmer Joe. Why does his head look like a rutabaga?"

The point is that life is a schlep, and it's easier to get through it with another ox.

YOU CAN ONLY YELL
AT ME FOR ONE THING
AT A TIME

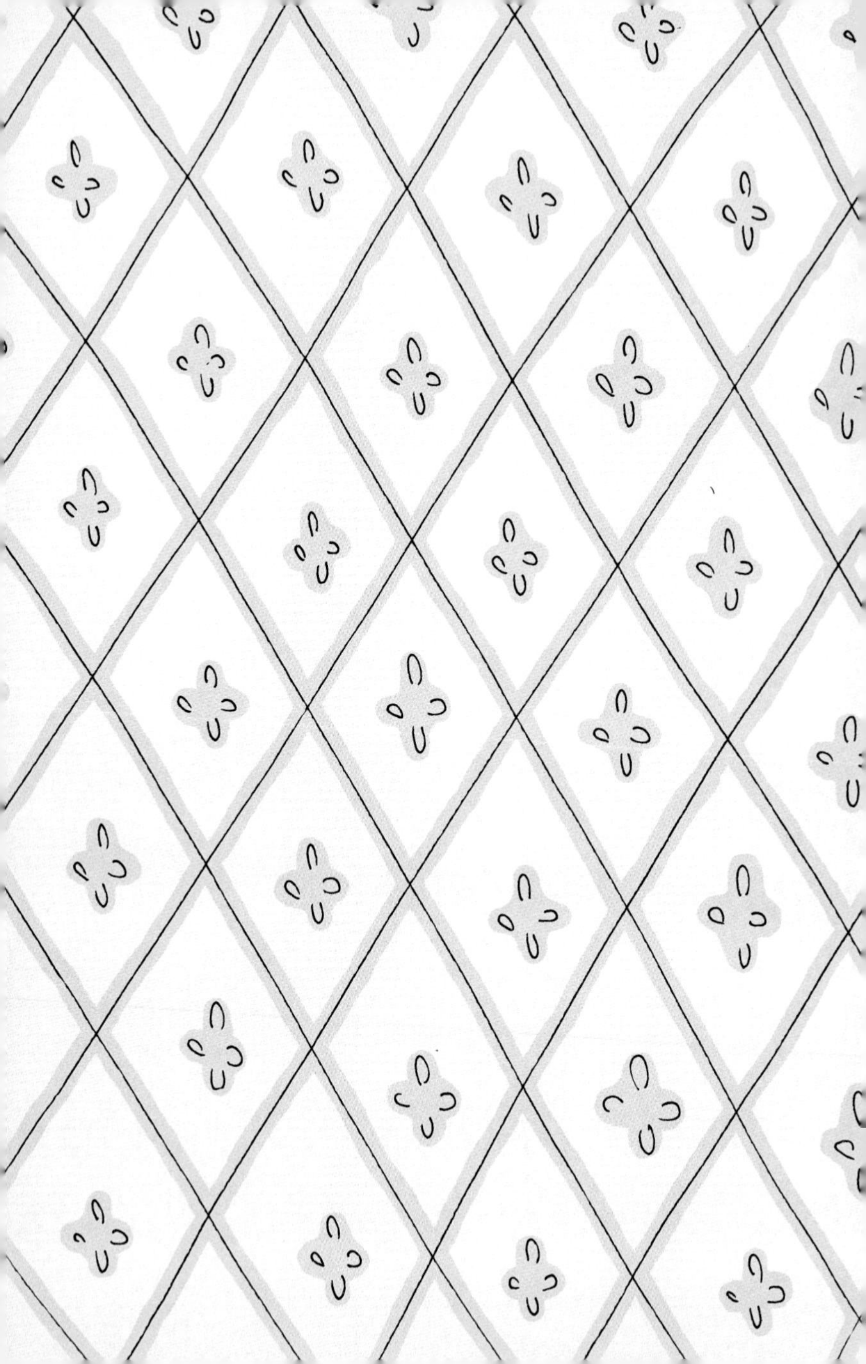

Sexual favors in exchange for cleaning up the cat vomit is a good and fair trade.

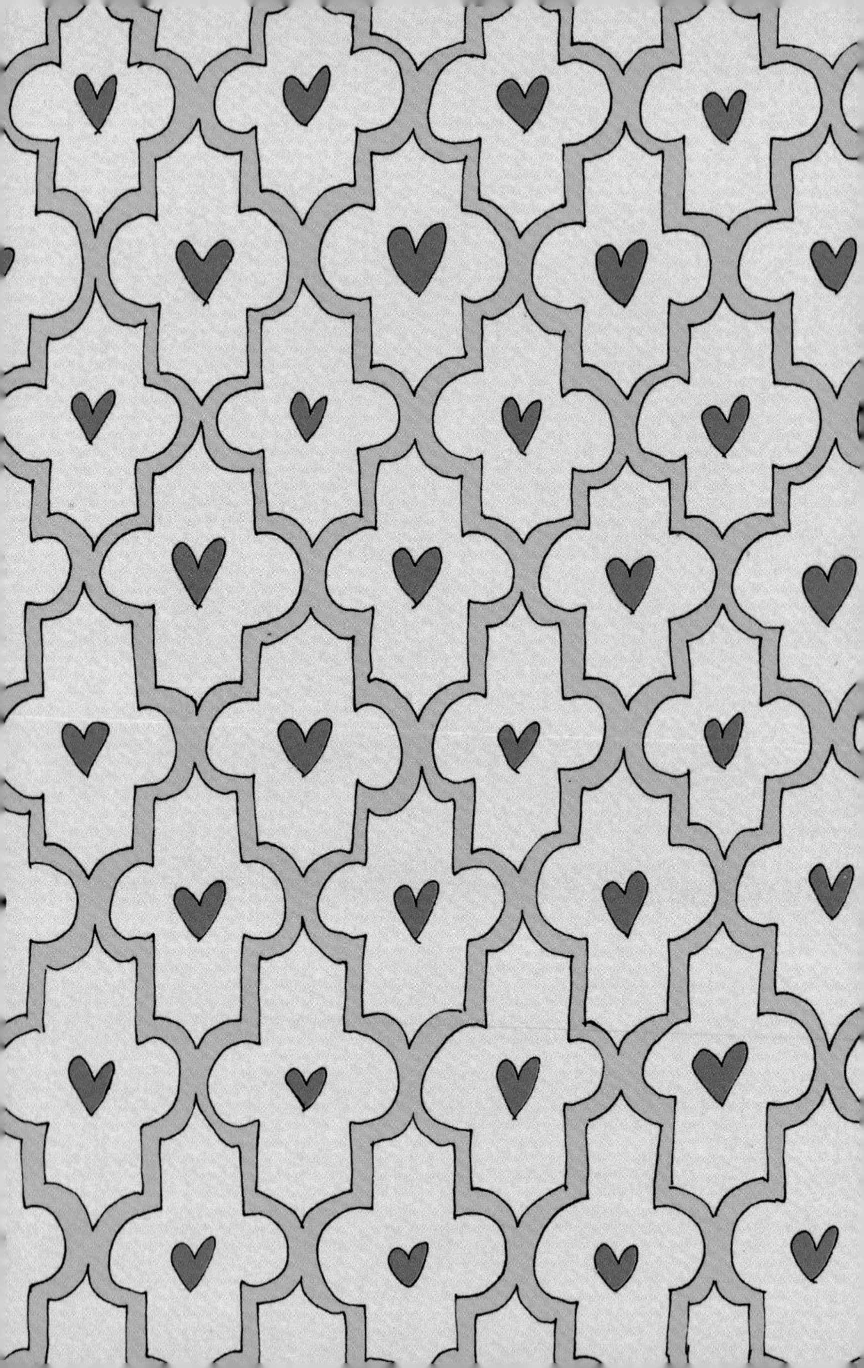

Queen-size beds, king-size blankets.

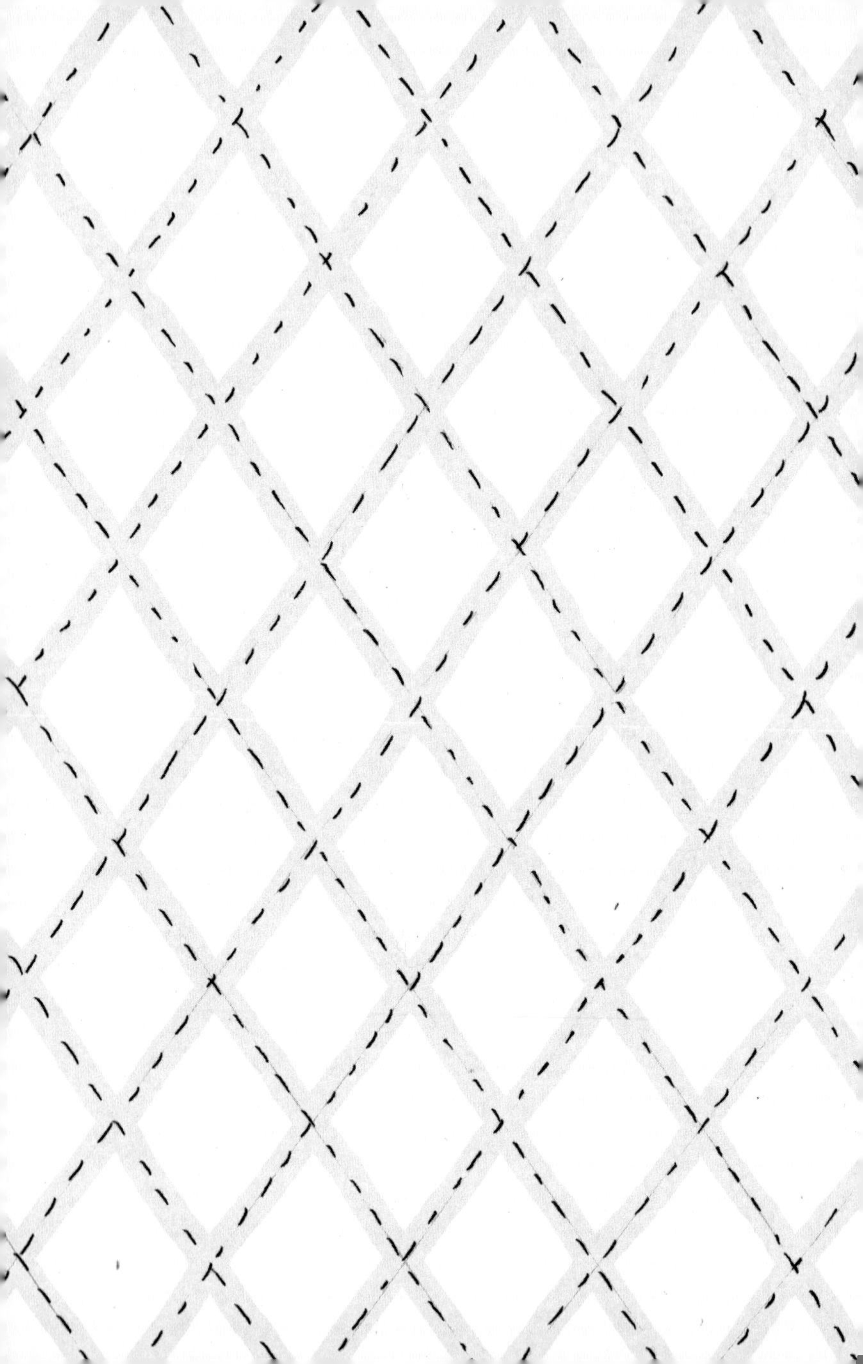

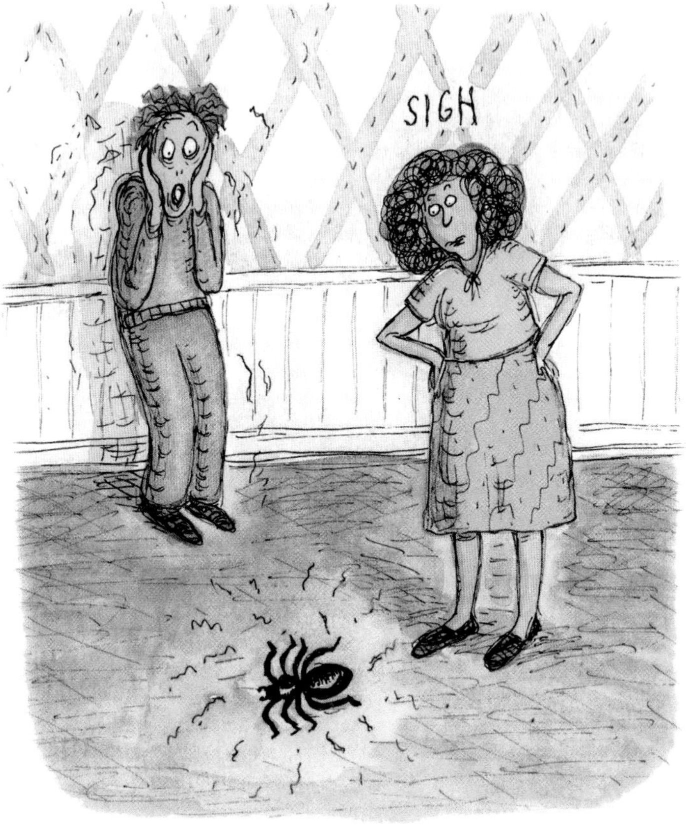
SIGH

If you are afraid of spiders, you should be with
someone who's good at dealing with them.

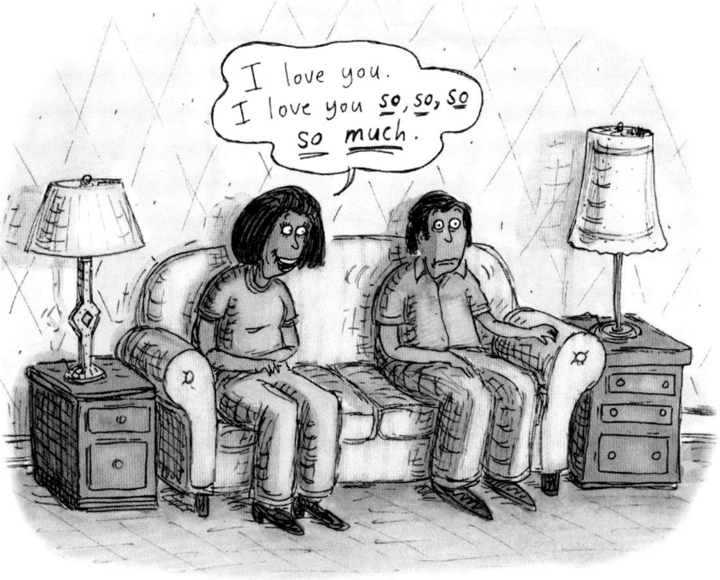
I love you.
I love you so, so, so
so much.

Force yourself to say "I love you." It makes the other person feel guilty and that always works to your advantage.

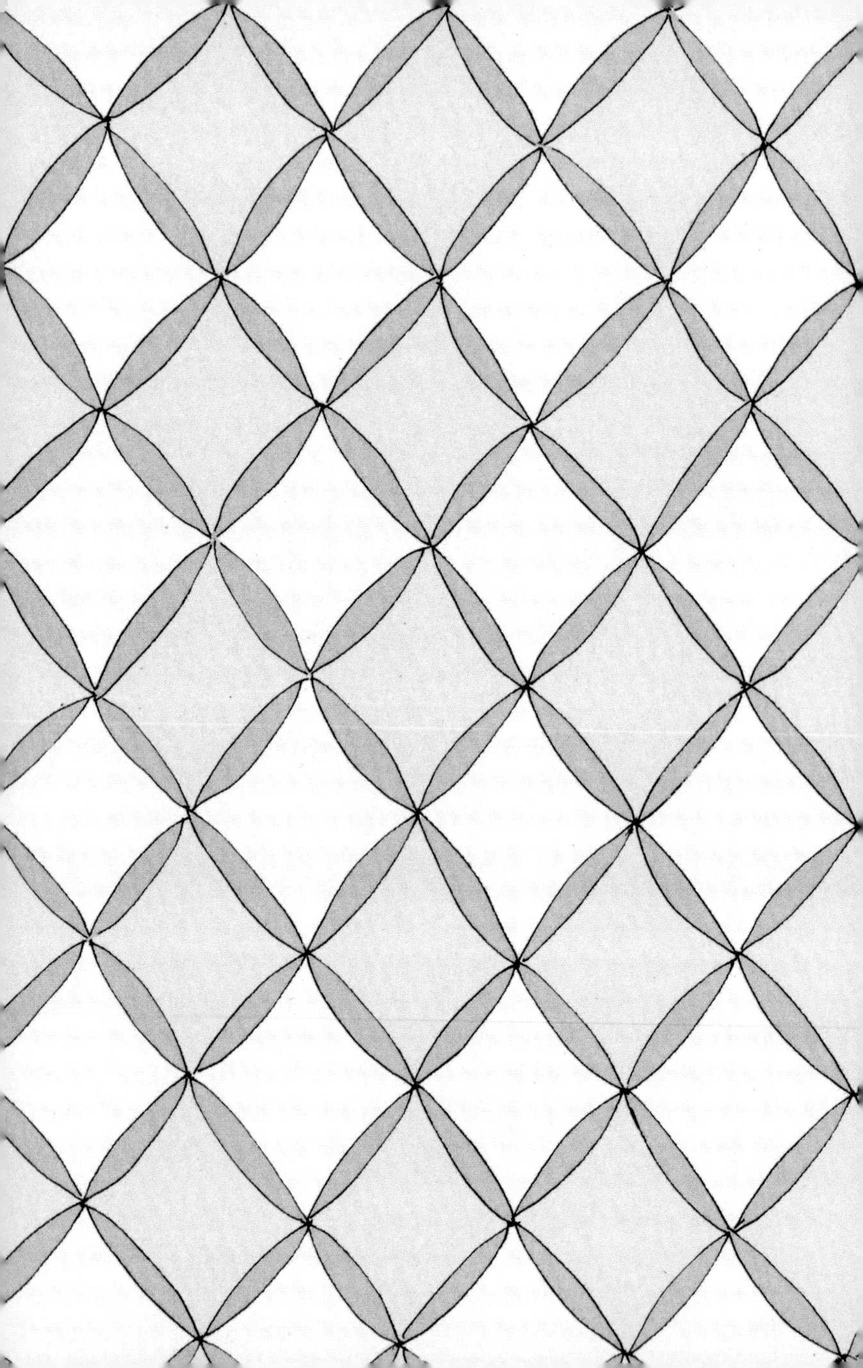

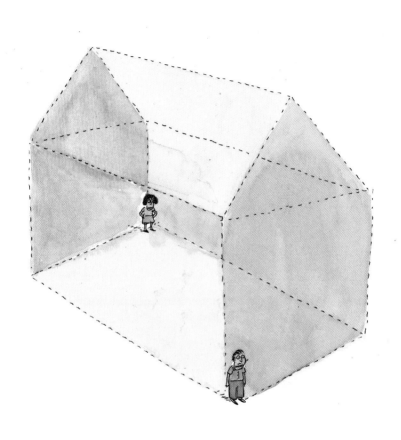

Live somewhere big enough that each of you
can think the other is dead.

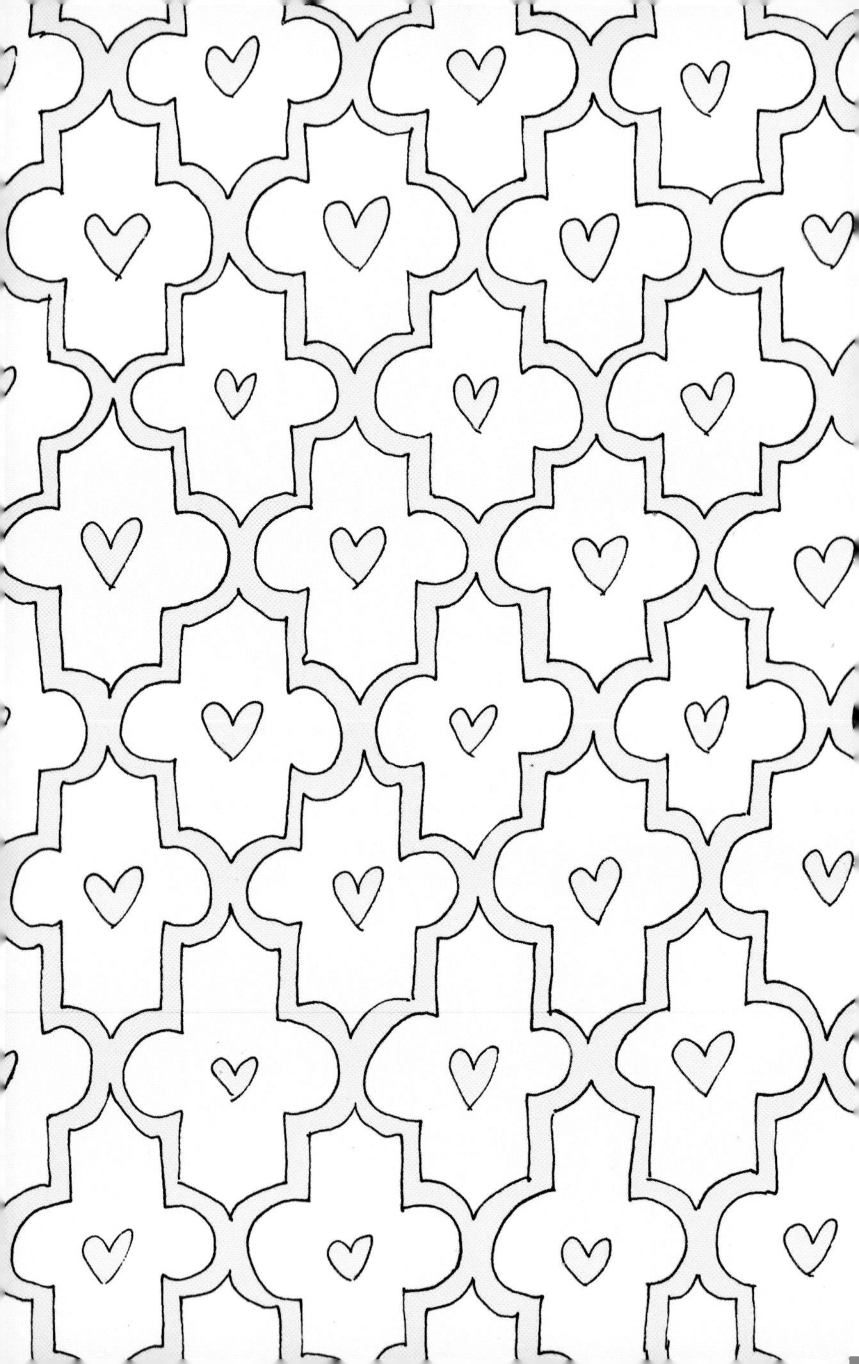

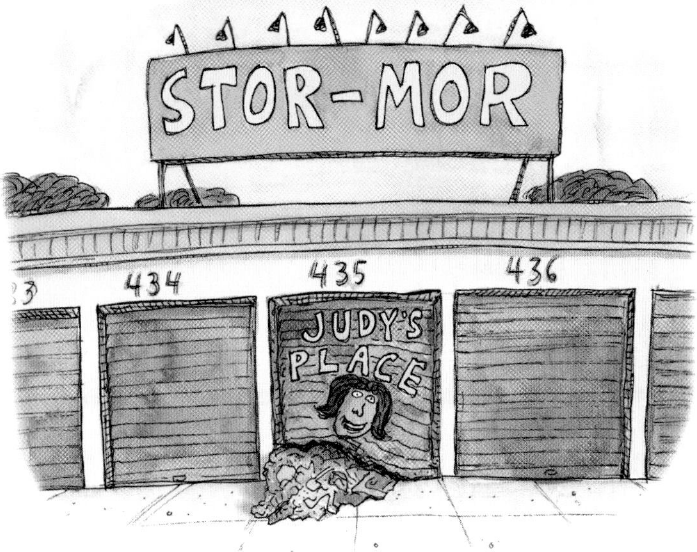
STOR-MOR
434
435
436
JUDY'S PLACE

If you keep buying stuff from Amazon ten times a day even though there's no more room in the house, you must buy a storage unit. And live in it.

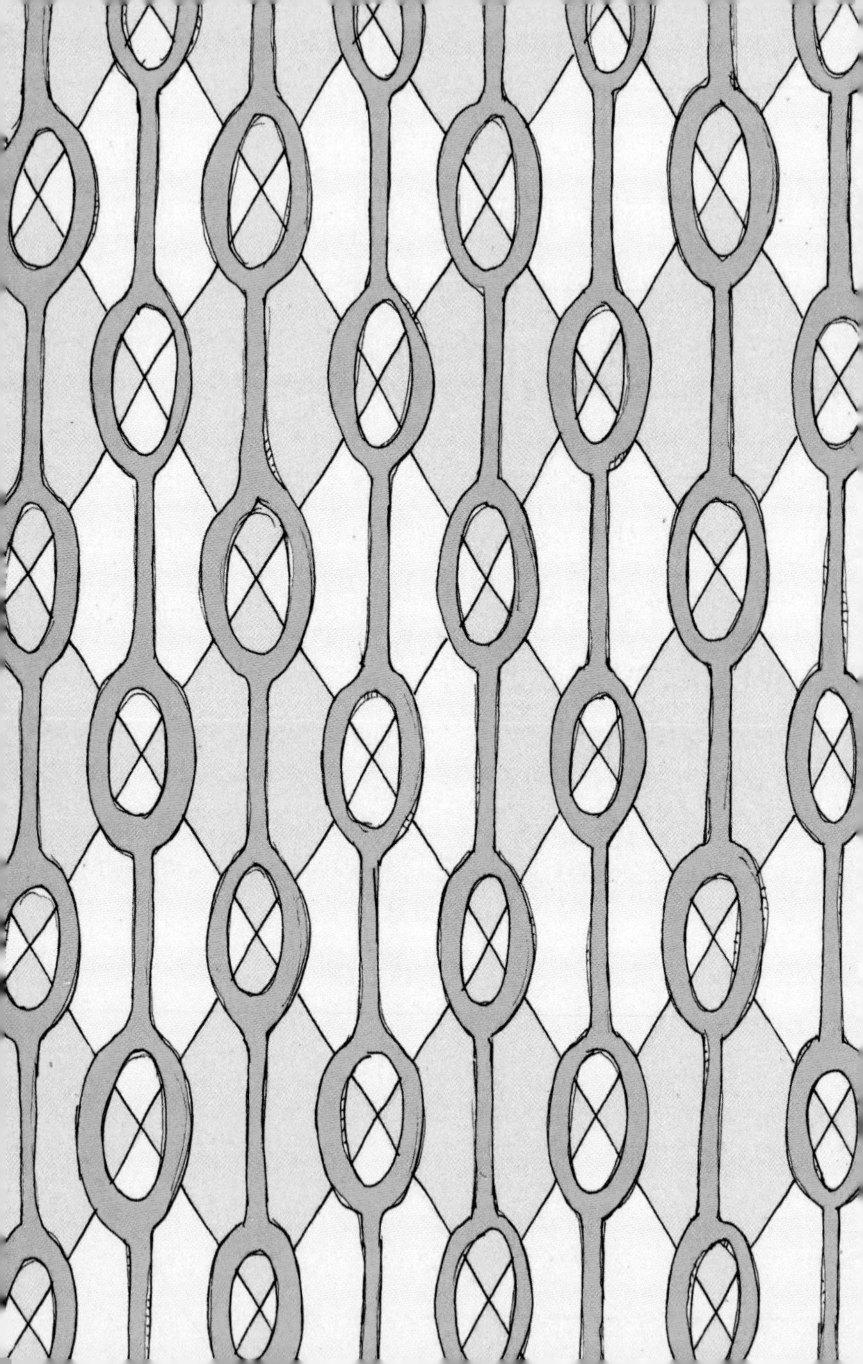

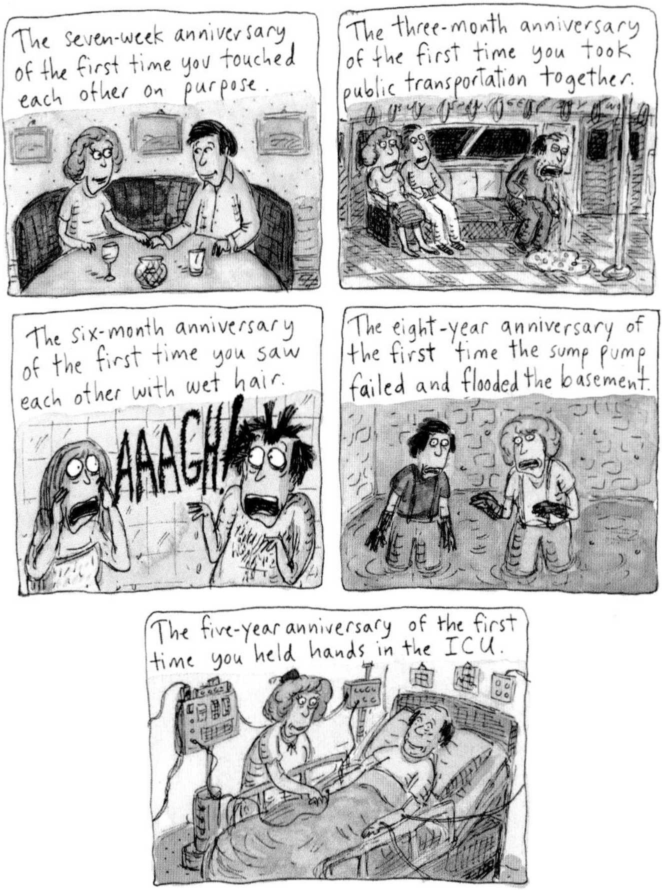
The seven-week anniversary of the first time you touched each other on purpose.
The three-month anniversary of the first time you took public transportation together.
The six-month anniversary of the first time you saw each other with wet hair.
AAAGH!
The eight-year anniversary of the first time the sump pump failed and flooded the basement.
The five-year anniversary of the first time you held hands in the ICU.

Celebrate the little things. . . .

Do not walk ten feet ahead of me
unless you are checking for land mines.

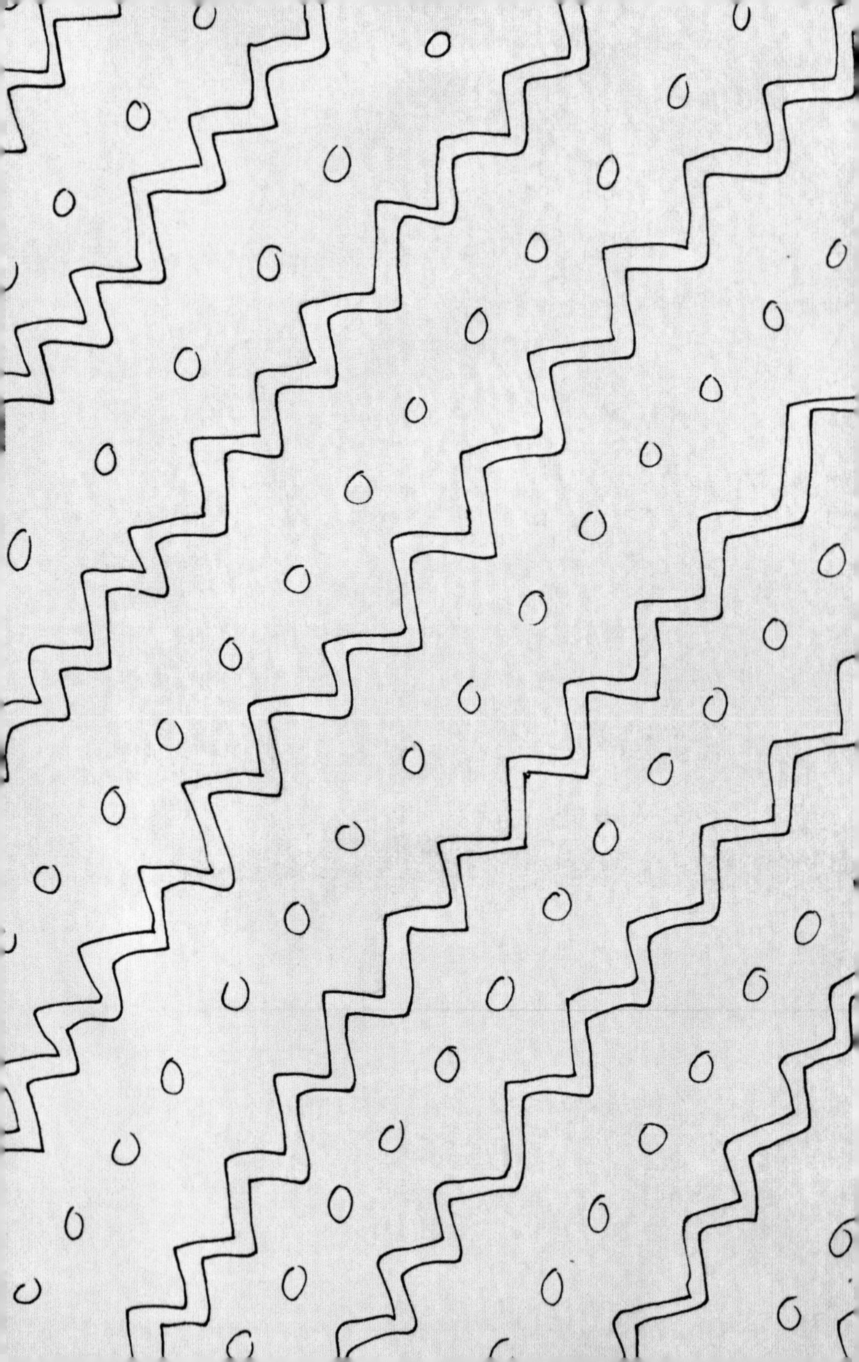

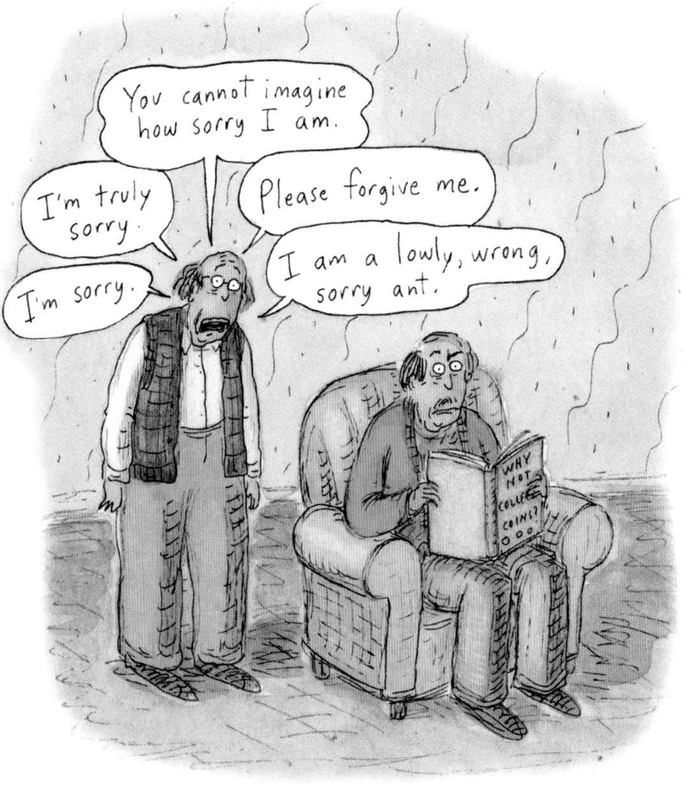
You cannot imagine how sorry I am.
I'm truly sorry.
Please forgive me.
I'm sorry.
I am a lowly, wrong, sorry ant.
WHY NOT
COINS?

When you do something wrong and there's no fixing it, apologize twenty times a day for being such a dick and soon I will become so sick and tired of hearing you babble, you will be forgiven.

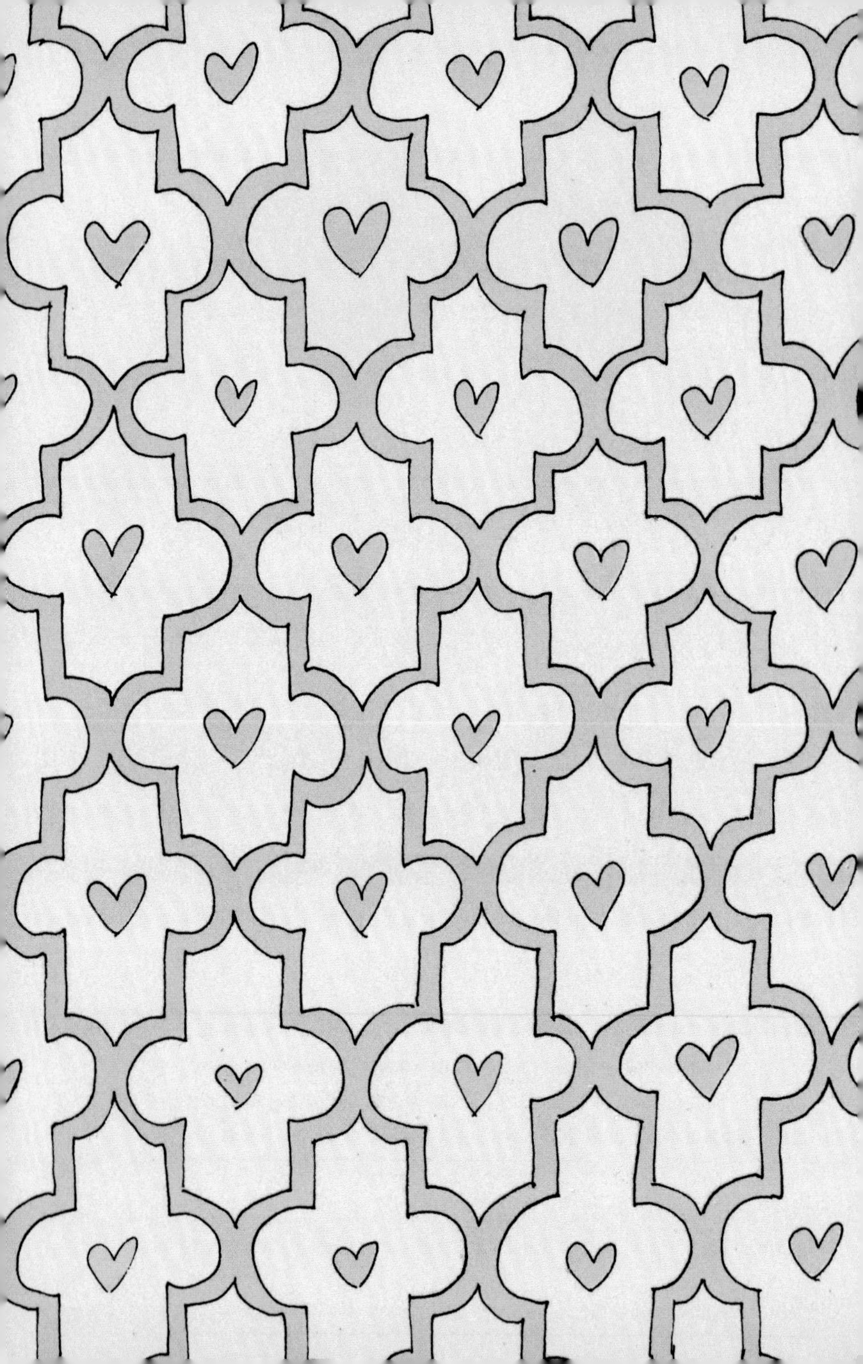

Adultery Day! The first Tuesday of every month,
you can pretend to be single. Wednesday,
no questions asked.

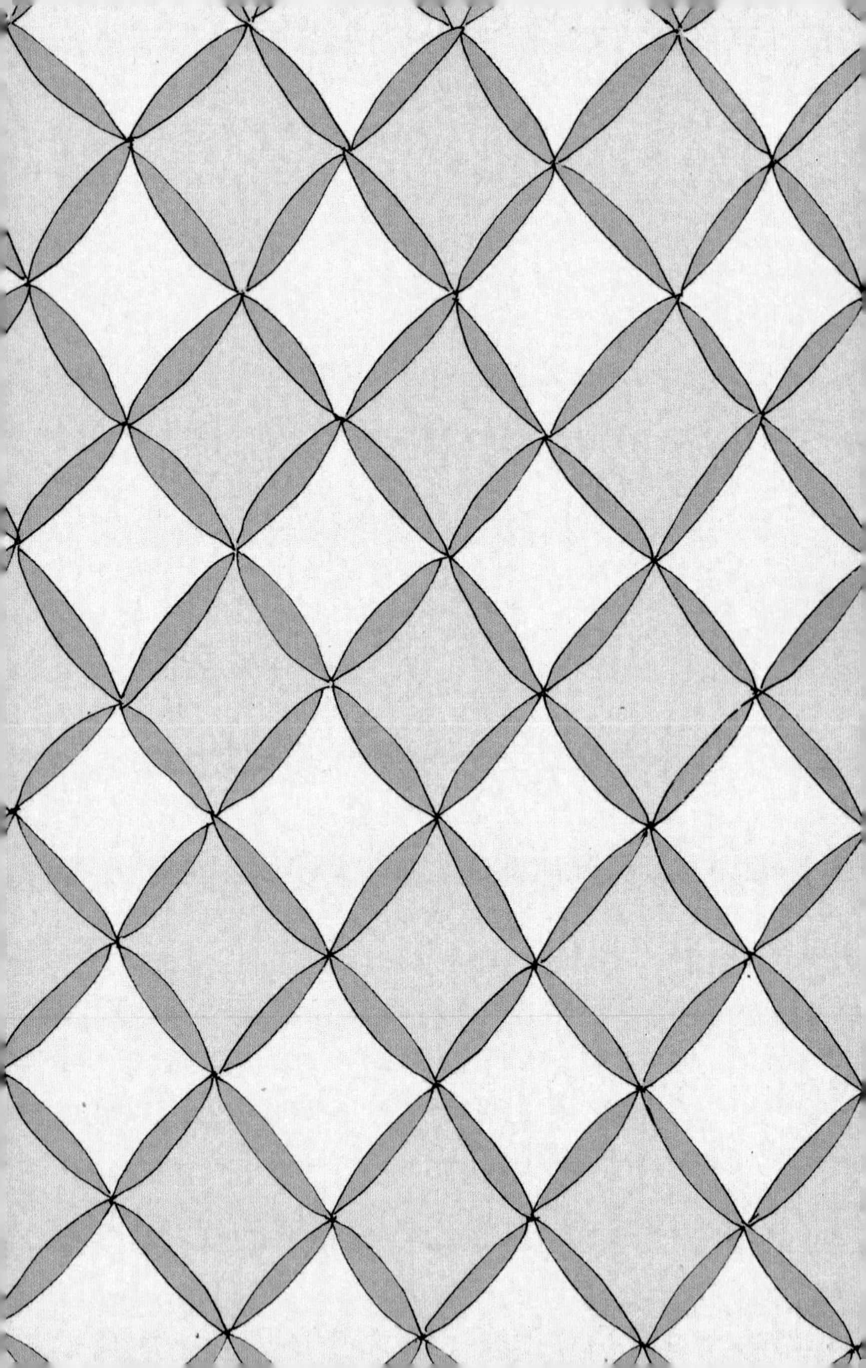

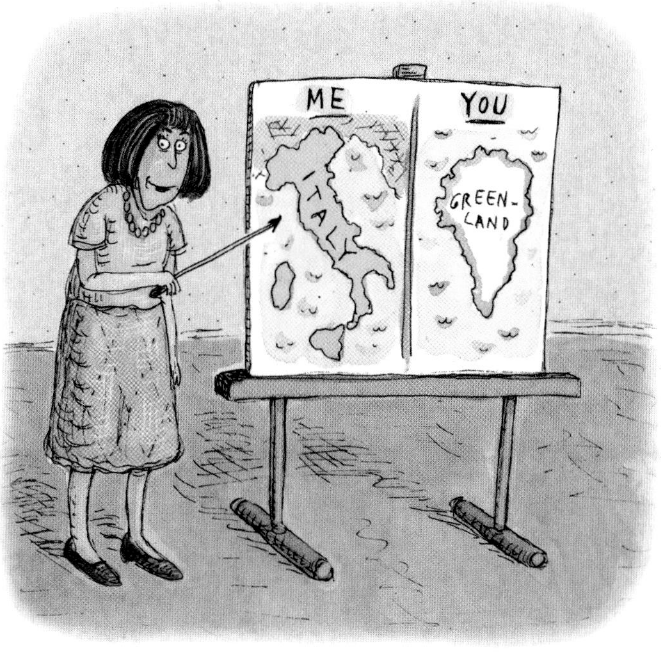
ME
YOU
ITALY
GREEN-
LAND

When separate bedrooms and freezer drawers
aren't enough, try separate countries.

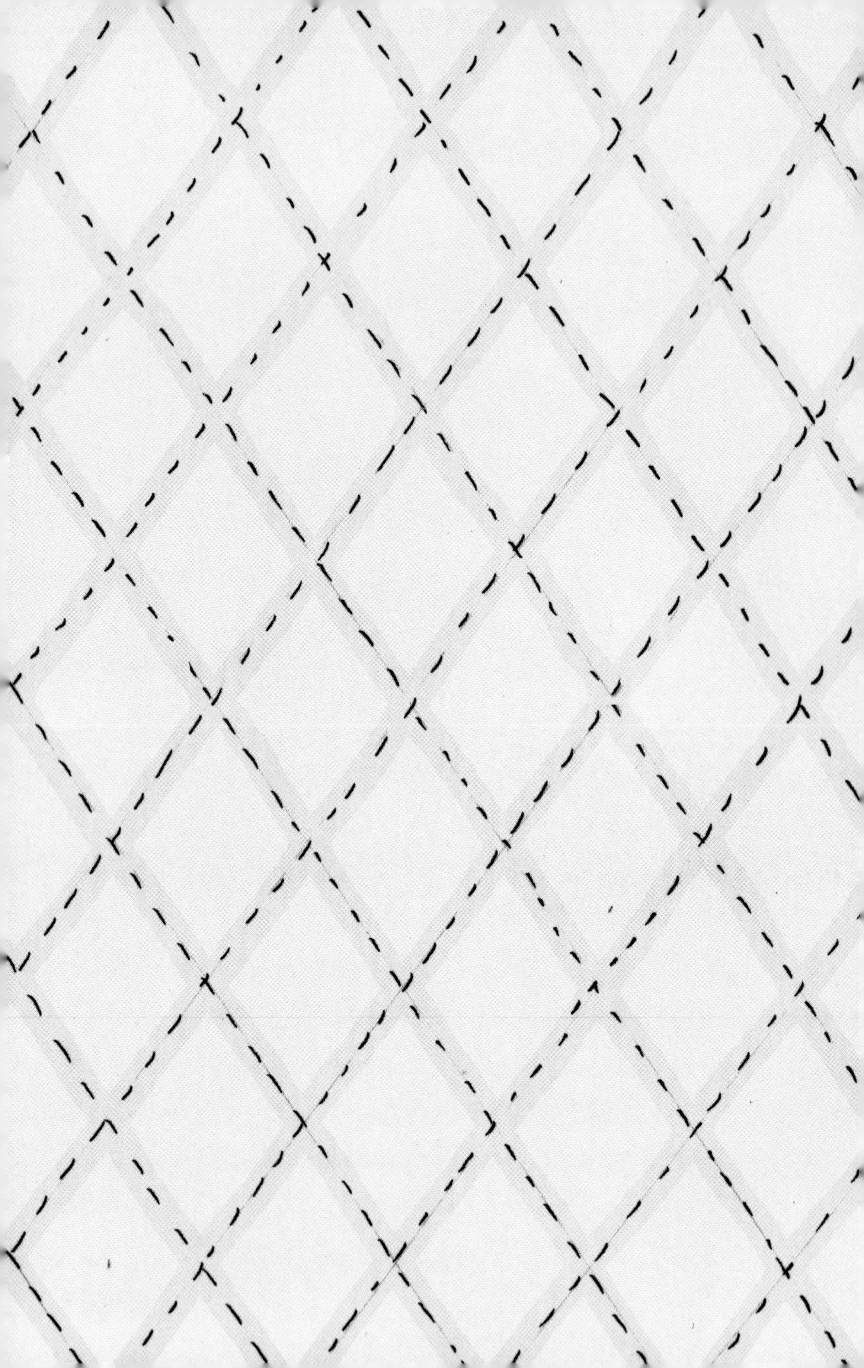

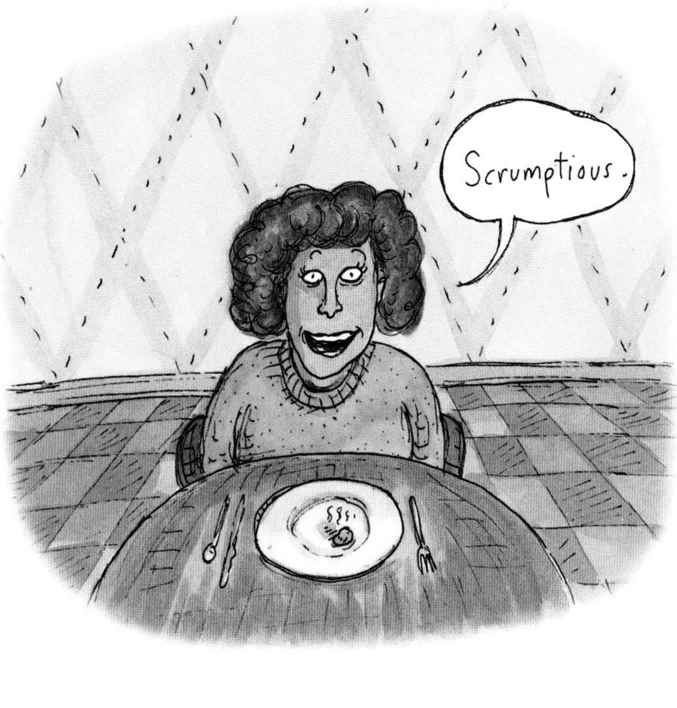
Scrumptious.

If I spend the day concocting an elaborate dish,
you must take a bite. If you spit it out,
you must still compliment me.

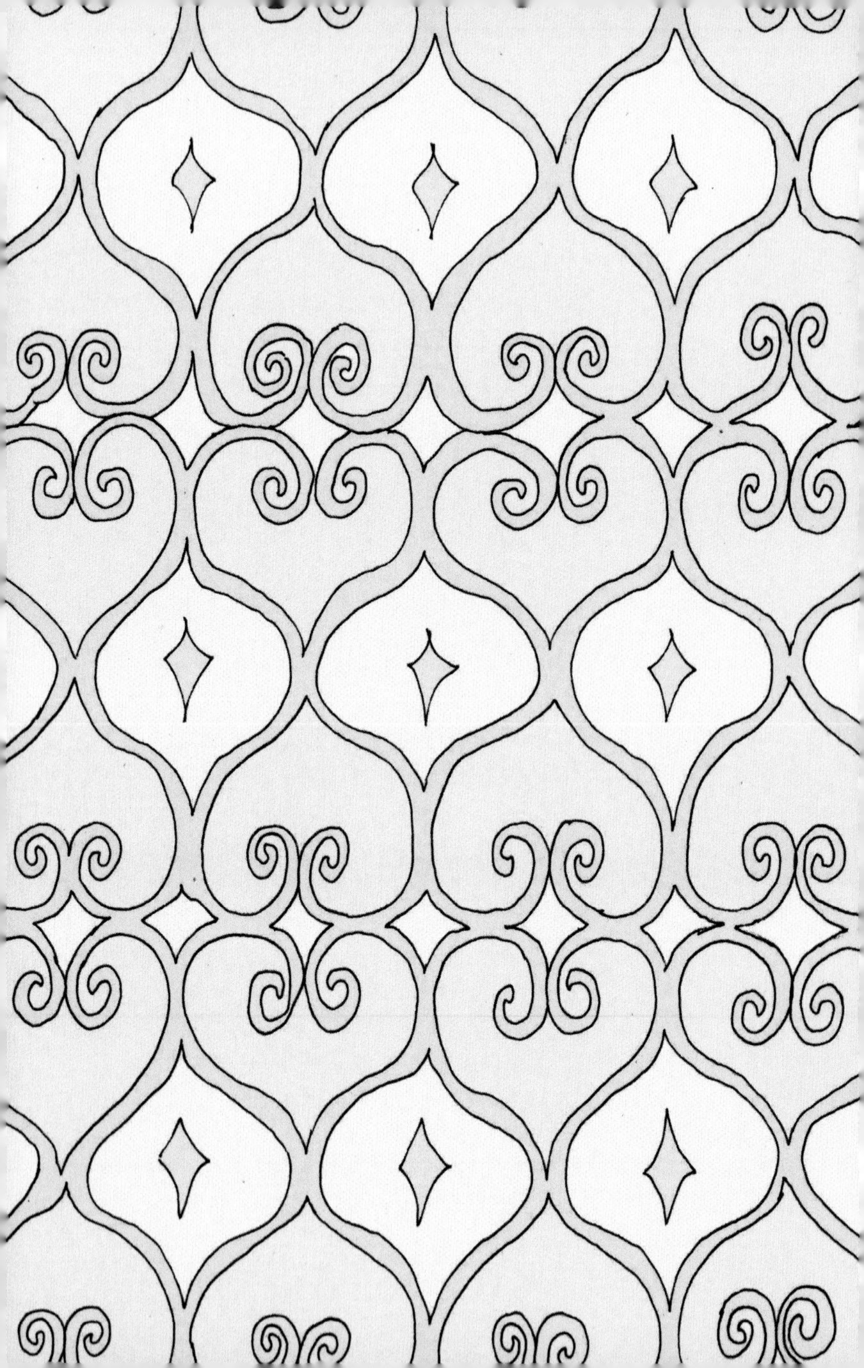

"My assistant"   "Emergency contact"   "Cracker Barrel"

"Garfunkel"   "Ben-Hur"   "Pimentos"

"Giblet"   "Lil Advil"   "Bodoni Bold"

Come up with tender names for each other. . . .

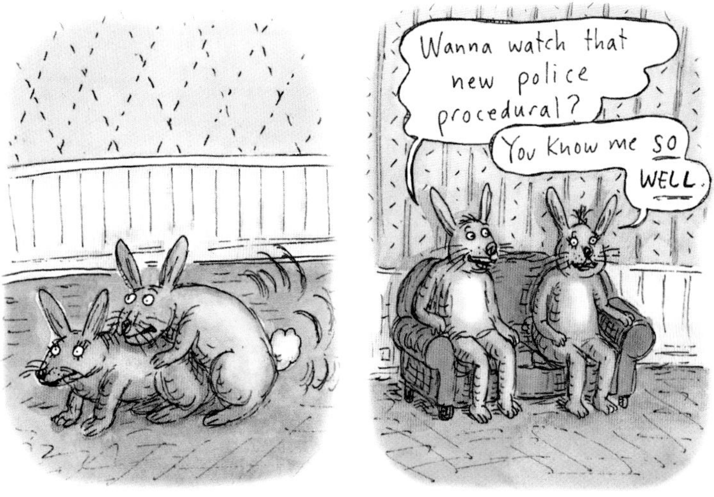
Wanna watch that new police procedural?
You know me SO WELL.

Sex constantly. Never have sex again.

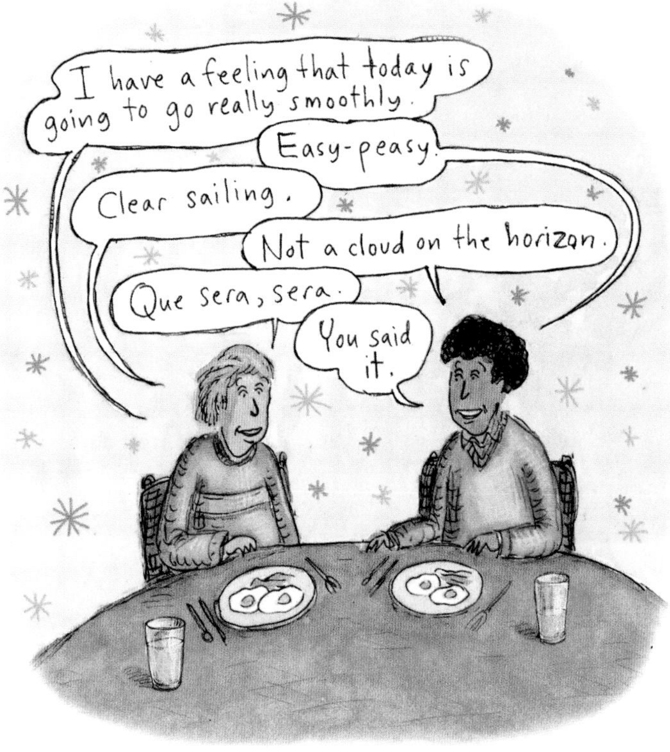
I have a feeling that today is going to go really smoothly.
Easy-peasy!
Clear sailing.
Not a cloud on the horizon.
Que sera, sera.
You said it.

Spike the orange juice with CBD oil.

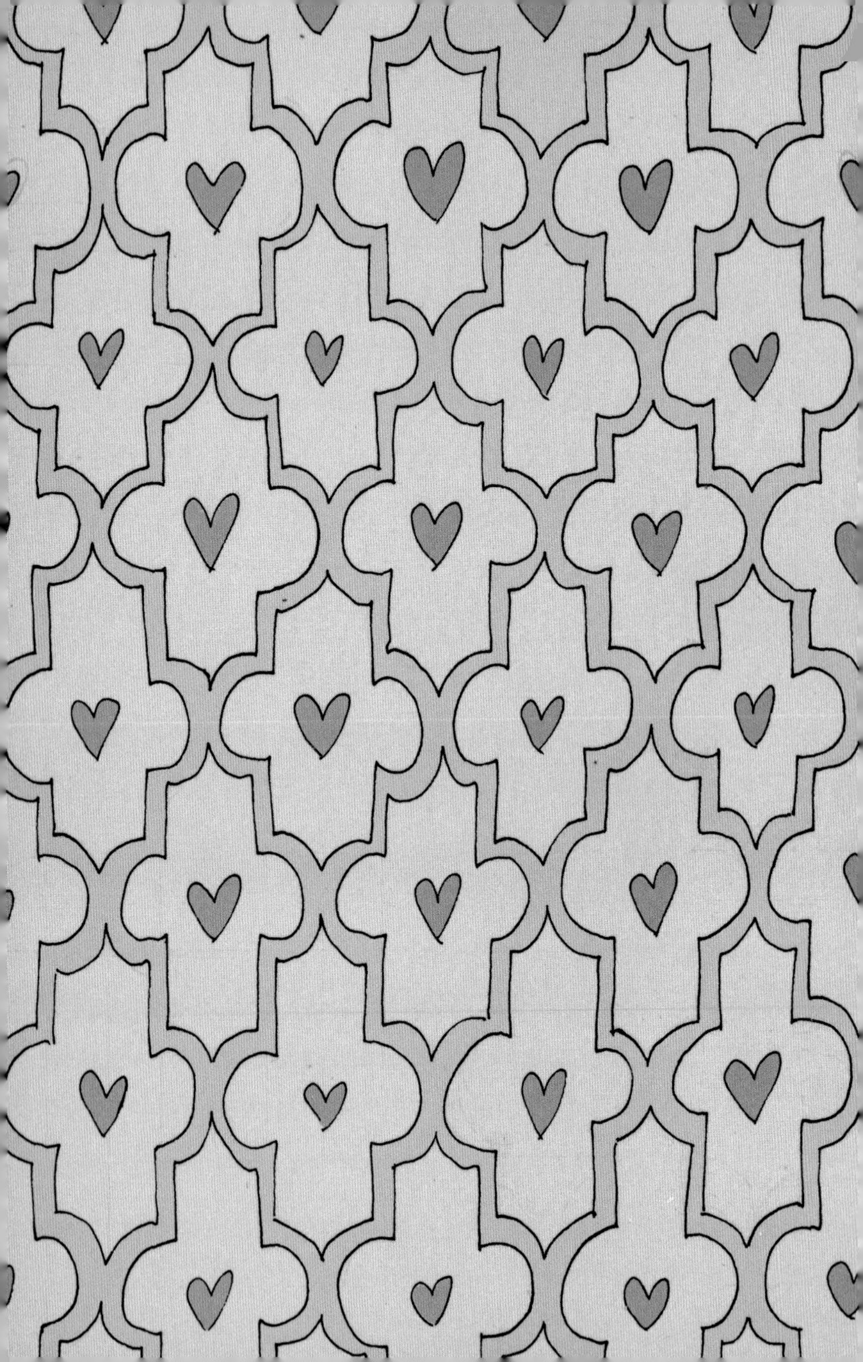

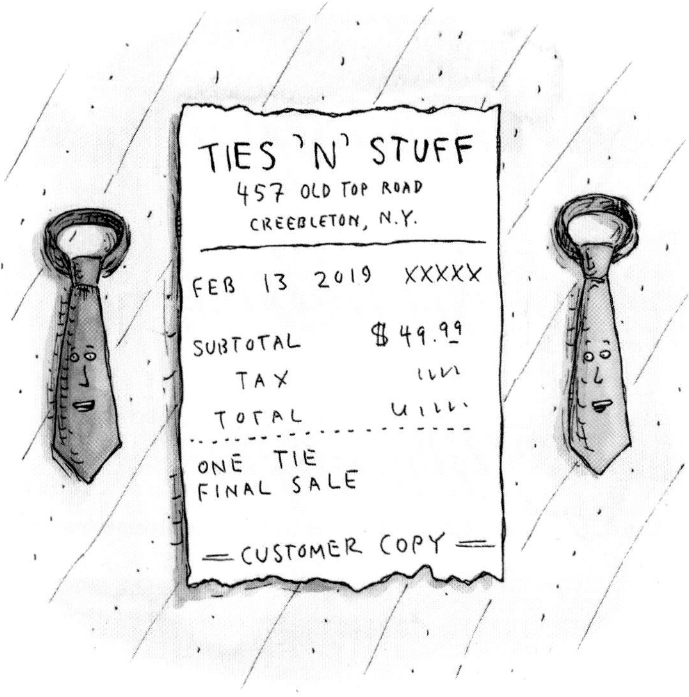
TIES 'N' STUFF
457 OLD TOP ROAD
CREEBLETON, N.Y.
FEB 13 2019 XXXXX
SUBTOTAL $49.99
TAX
TOTAL
ONE TIE
FINAL SALE
CUSTOMER COPY

If you buy an expensive Valentine's Day gift, save the receipt. You might need it to prove how generous you are.

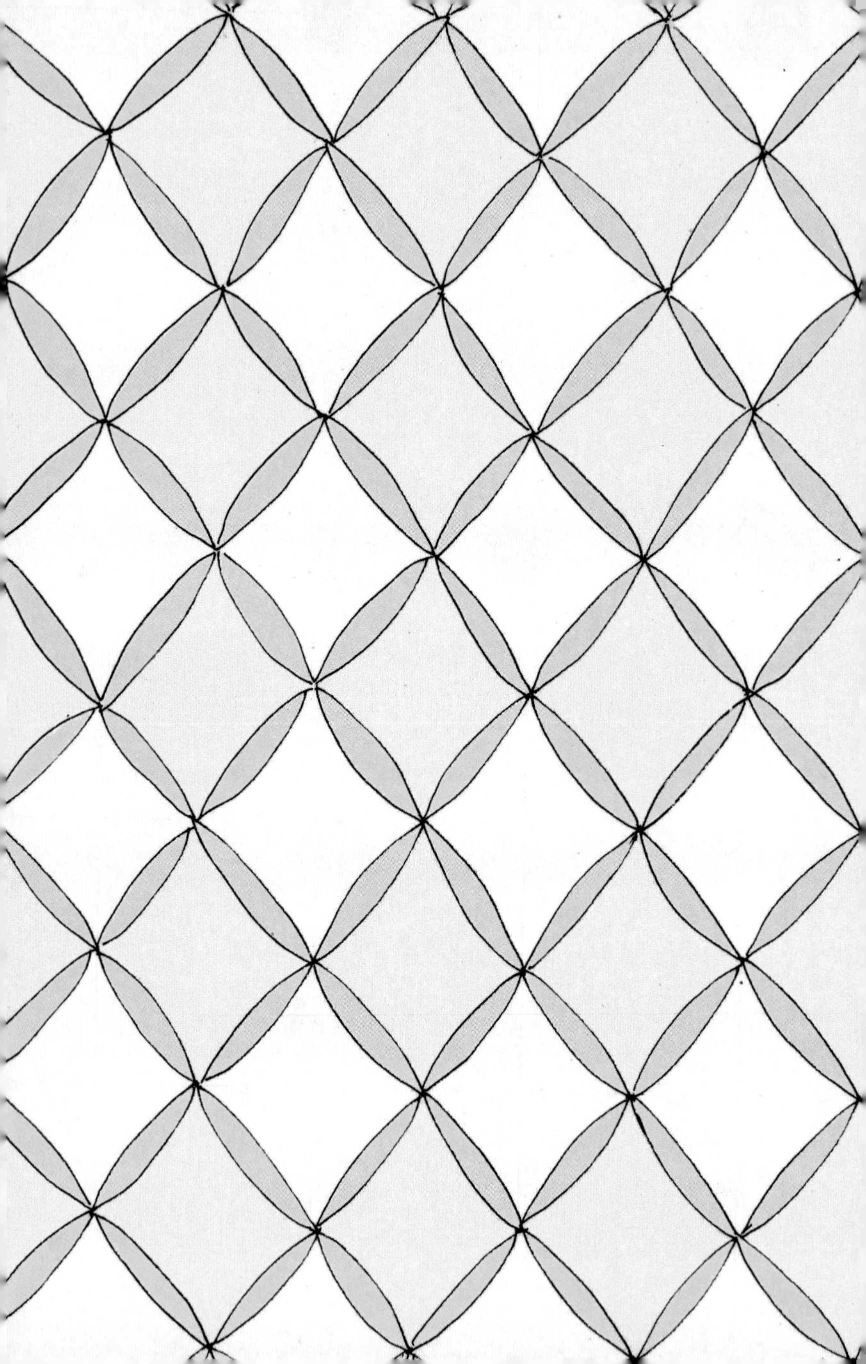

It is easier to stay inside and wait for the snow to
melt than to fight about who should shovel.

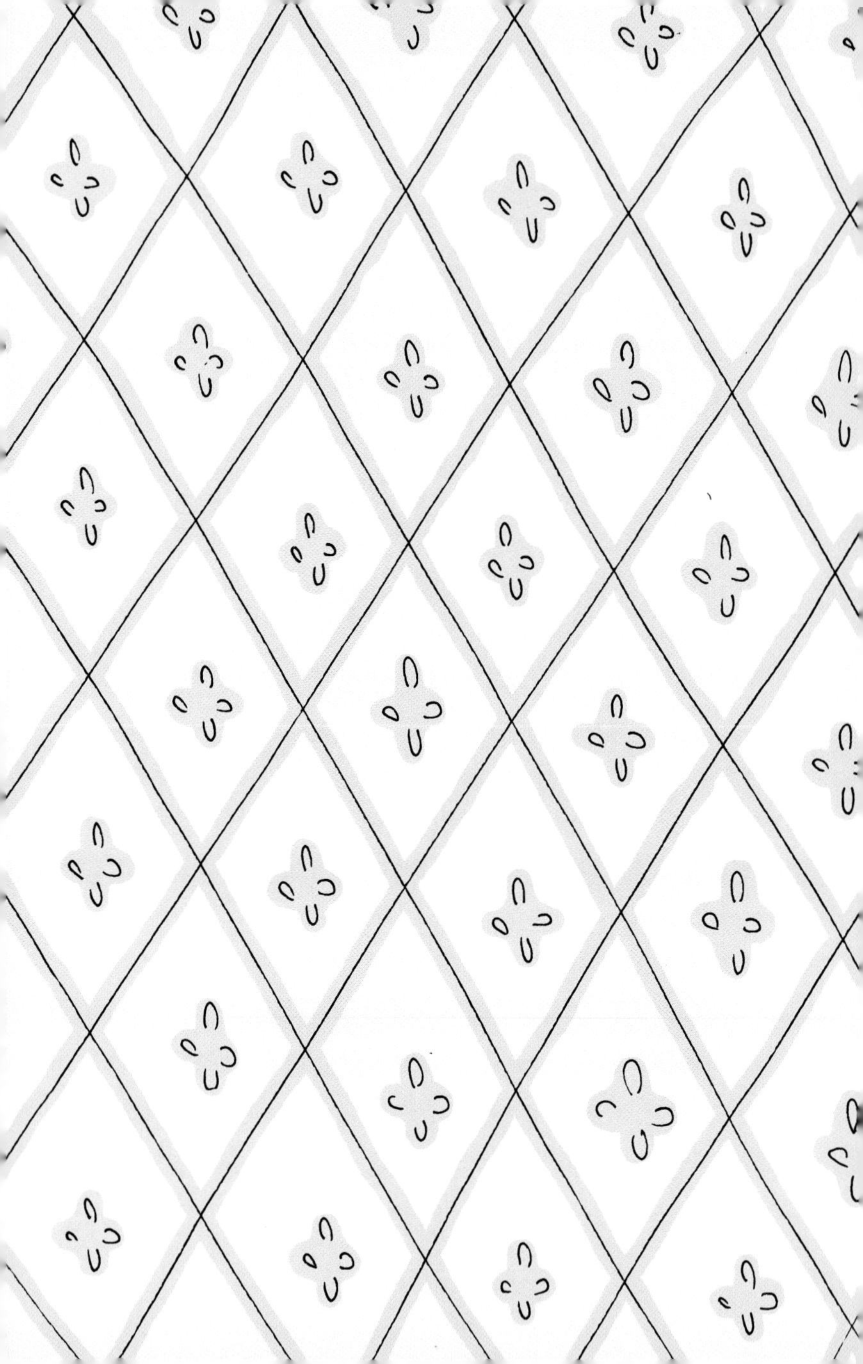

One of us better learn how to fold a fitted sheet.
Or else we should invite Martha Stewart
to be our permanent houseguest.

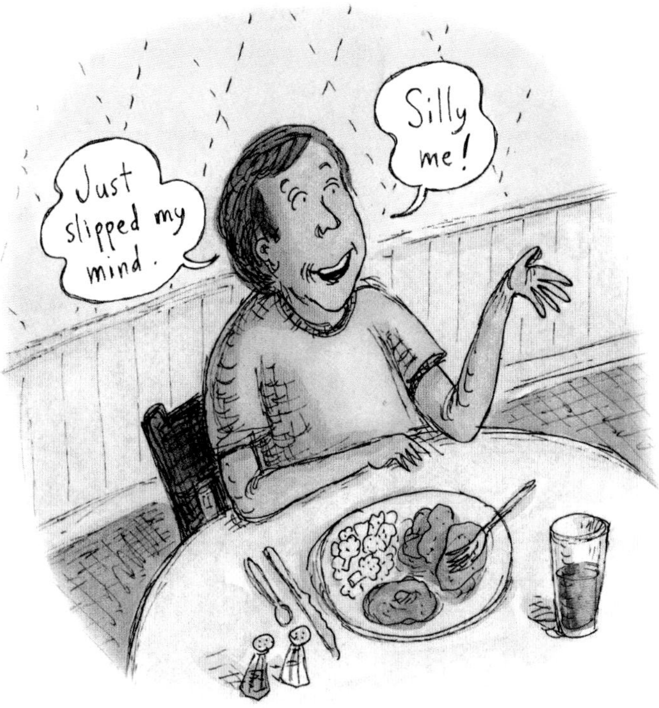
Just slipped my mind.
Silly me!

If one person spent the entire afternoon grocery shopping and cooking for a meal we both agreed would start at 7:00, the other person cannot take a nibble of cauliflower, explaining, "I had a burger and milkshake at 3:30 at Two Men and a Griddle."

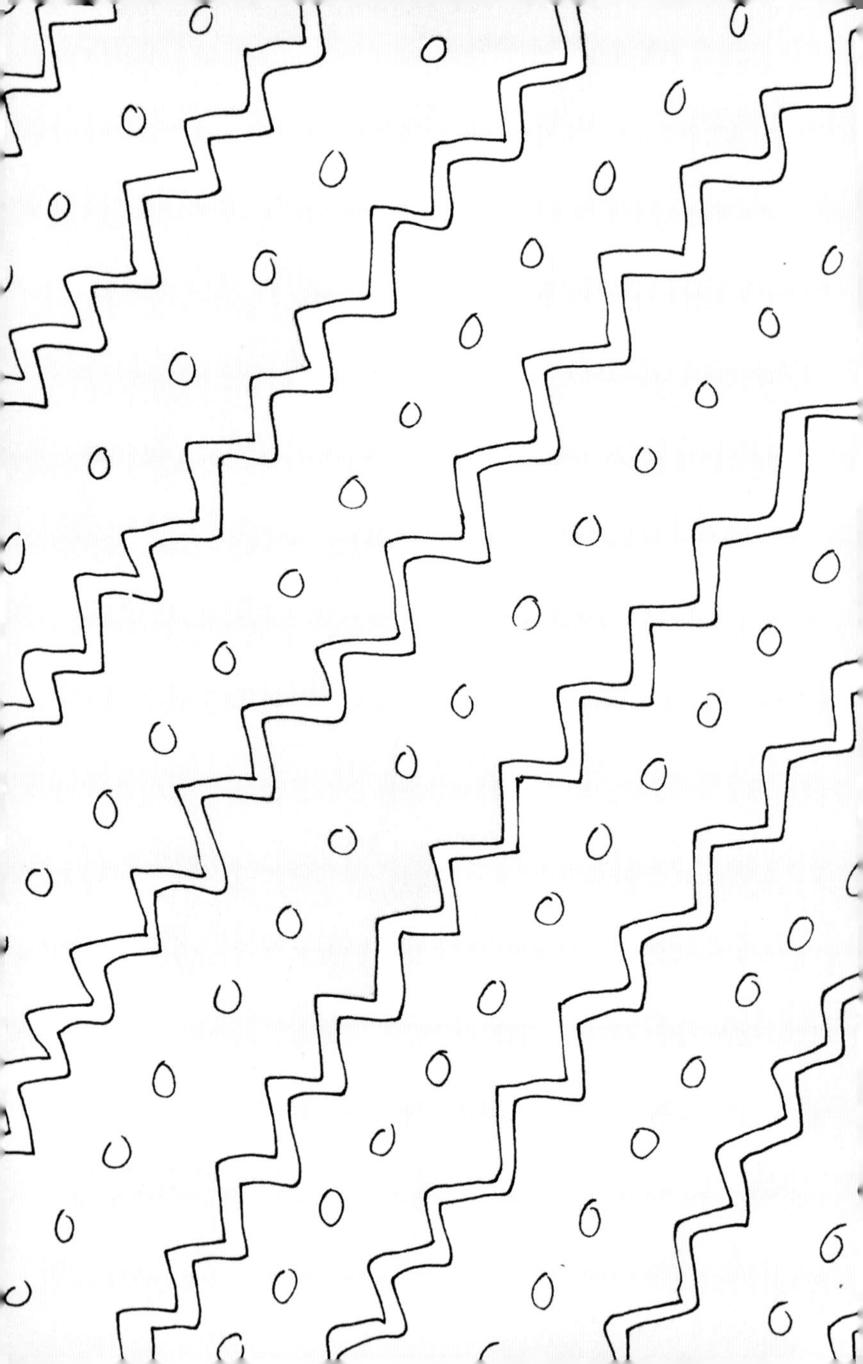

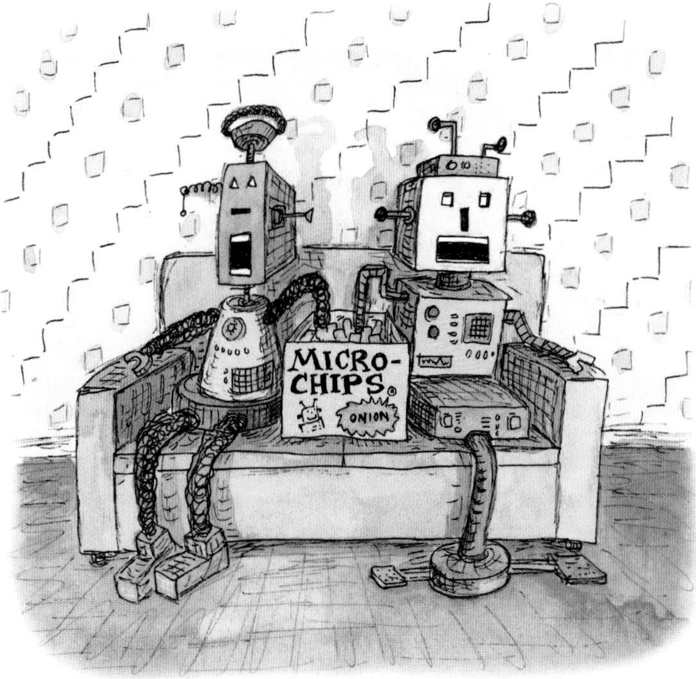
MICRO-
CHIPS®
ONION

Try to find someone whose taste in snacks
is compatible with yours.

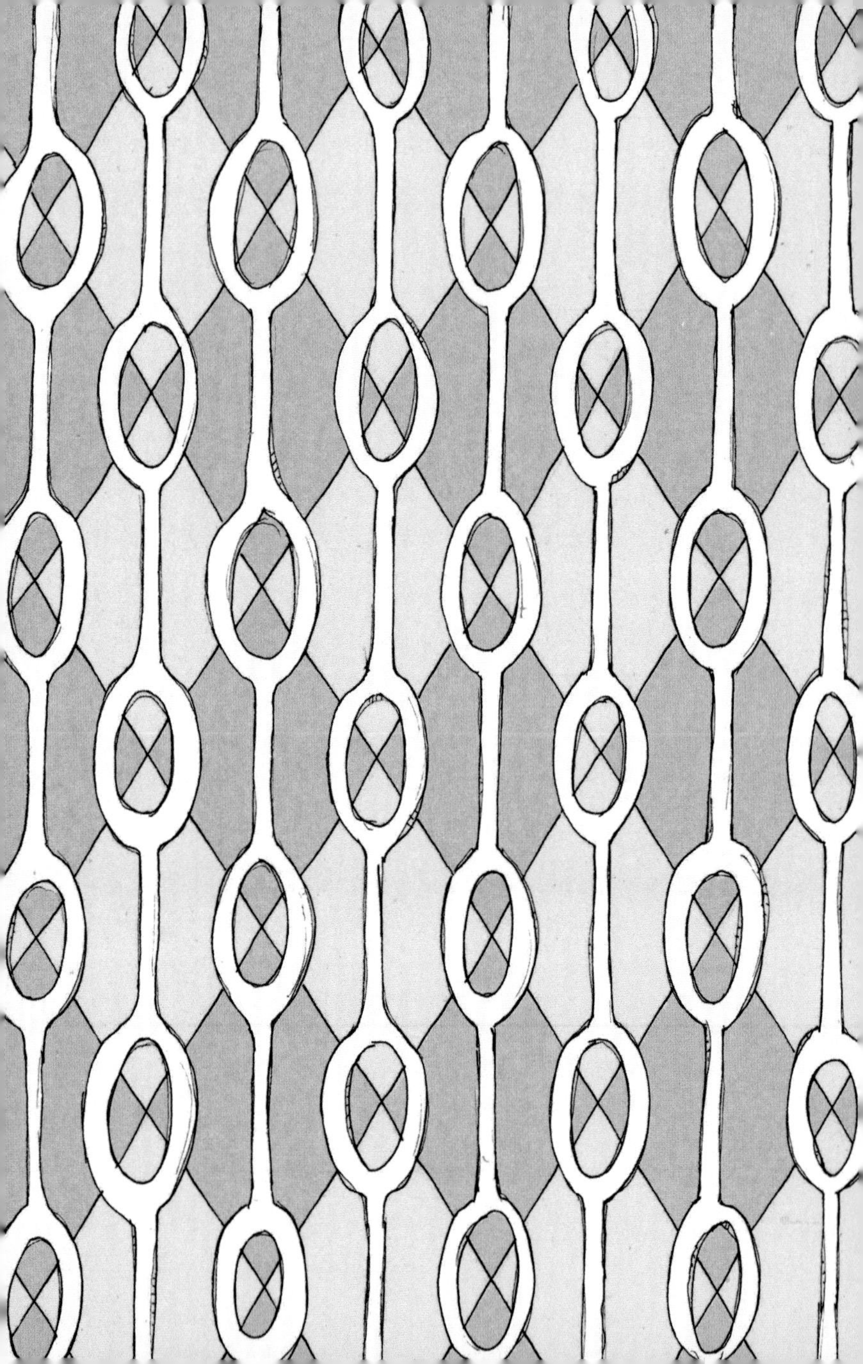

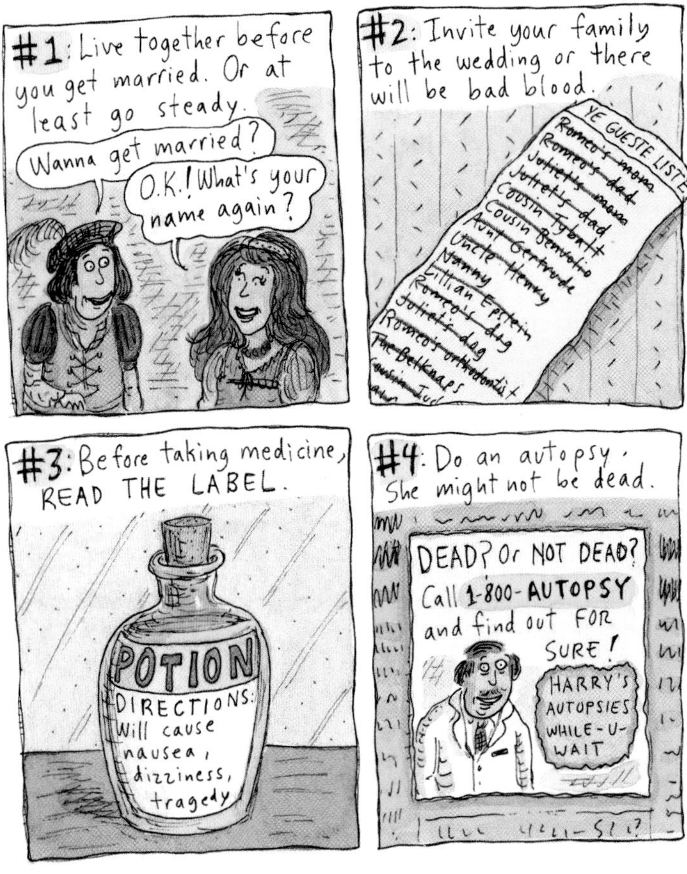
#1: Live together before you get married. Or at least go steady.
Wanna get married?
O.K.! What's your name again?
#2: Invite your family to the wedding or there will be bad blood.
YE GUESTE LISTE
Romeo's mom
Romeo's dad
Juliet's mom
Juliet's dad
Cousin Tybalt
Cousin Benvolio
Aunt Gertrude
Uncle Henry
Nanny
Lillian Epstein
Romeo's dog
Juliet's dog
Romeo's orthodontist
The Belknaps
#3: Before taking medicine, READ THE LABEL.
POTION
DIRECTIONS: Will cause nausea, dizziness, tragedy
#4: Do an autopsy. She might not be dead.
DEAD? Or NOT DEAD?
Call 1-800-AUTOPSY and find out FOR SURE!
HARRY'S AUTOPSIES WHILE-U-WAIT

Think "What would Romeo and Juliet do?"
Then do the opposite.

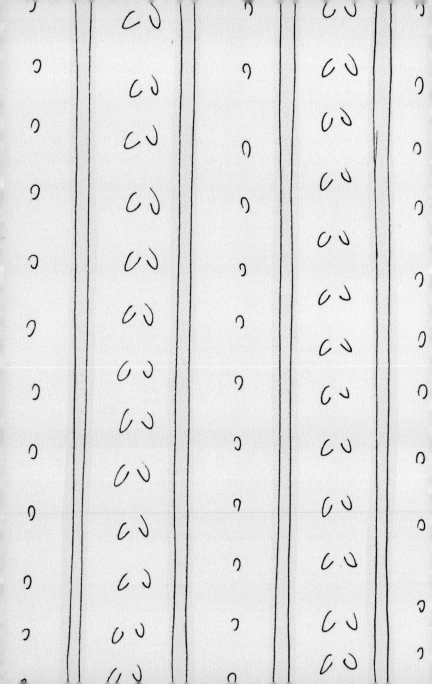

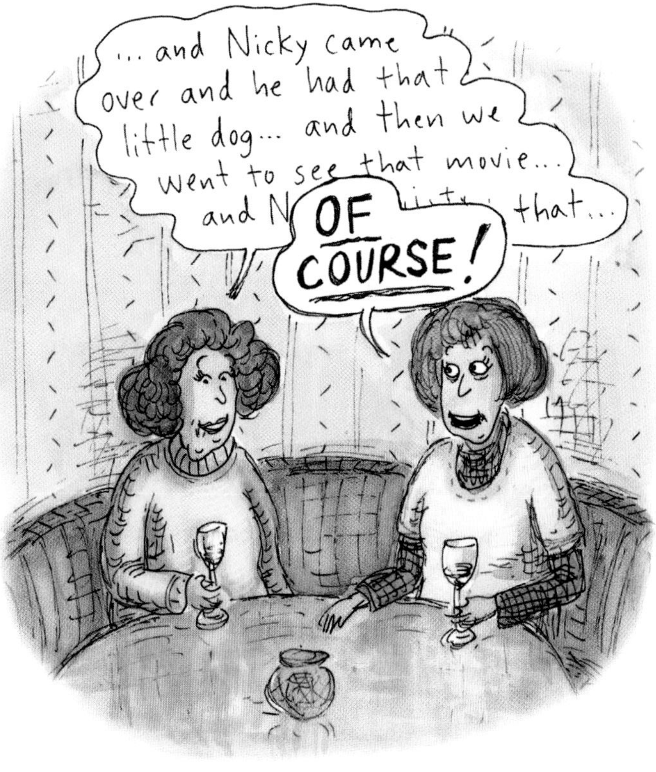

... and Nicky came over and he had that little dog... and then we went to see that movie... and N that...
OF COURSE!

The answer to the question "You know whatchamacallit who was dating the one with the father who had the business and there was that thing?" is yes.

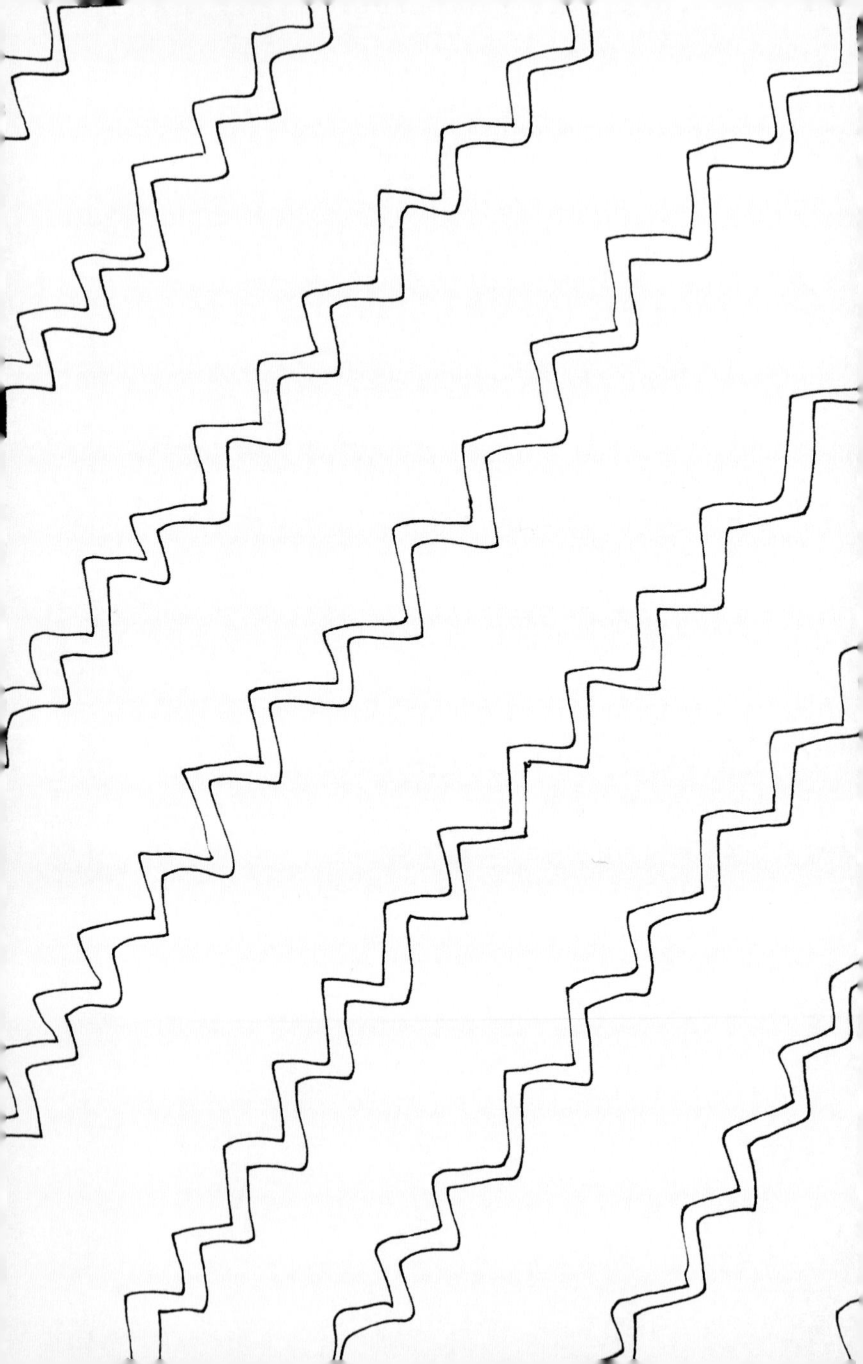

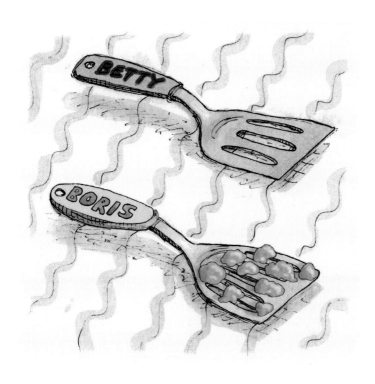

If you are unwilling to clean the spatula
after you use it, get your own.

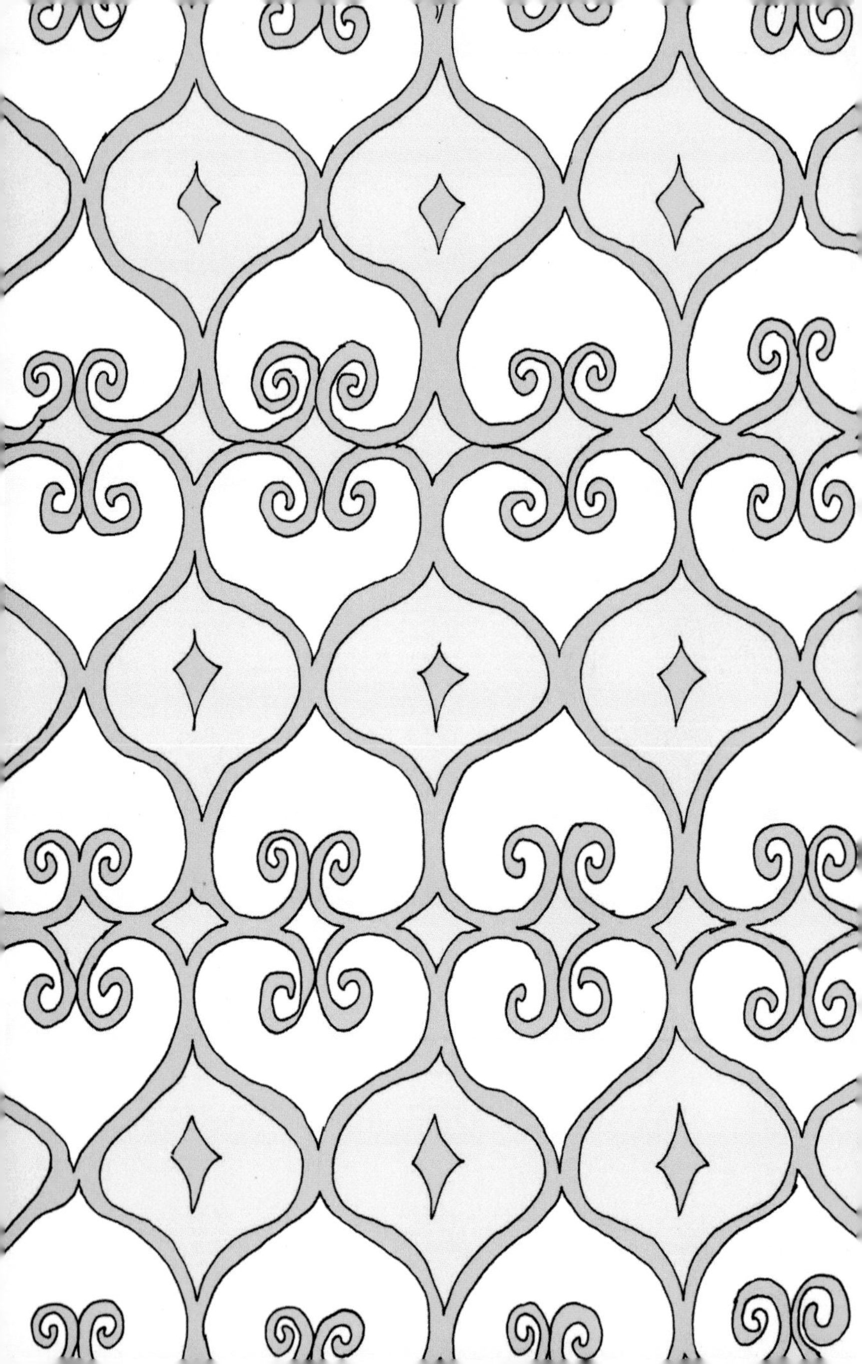

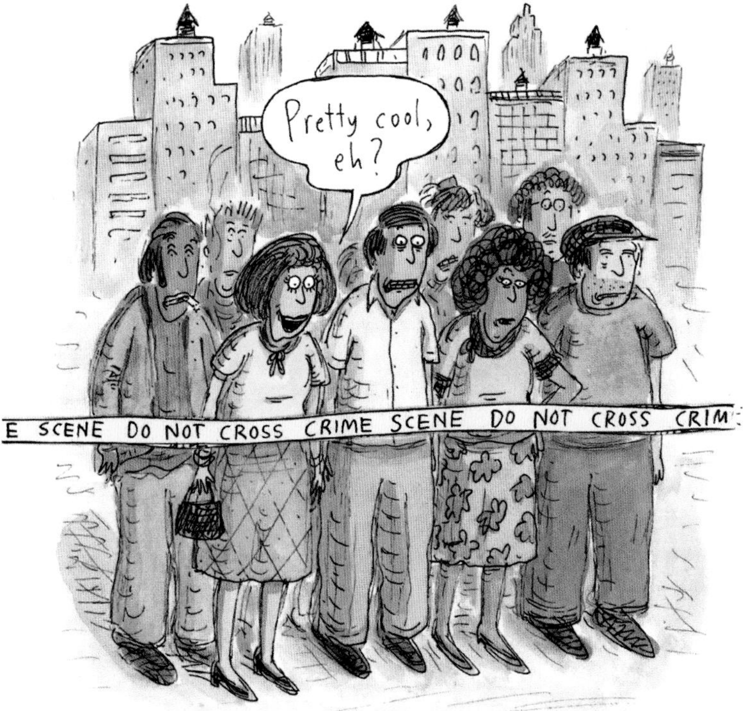
Pretty cool, eh?
E SCENE DO NOT CROSS CRIME SCENE DO NOT CROSS CRIM

Beware of anyone who takes you on a first date to a walk-in dermatology clinic. Or a crime scene.

"I can't WAIT to spend Thanksgiving with your family!"
"This looks delicious! Yum!"
"You're much handsomer than my ex. He reminds me too much of George Clooney."
"Eight rolls of masking tape! It's what I've always wanted!"

Honesty is not necessarily the best policy.

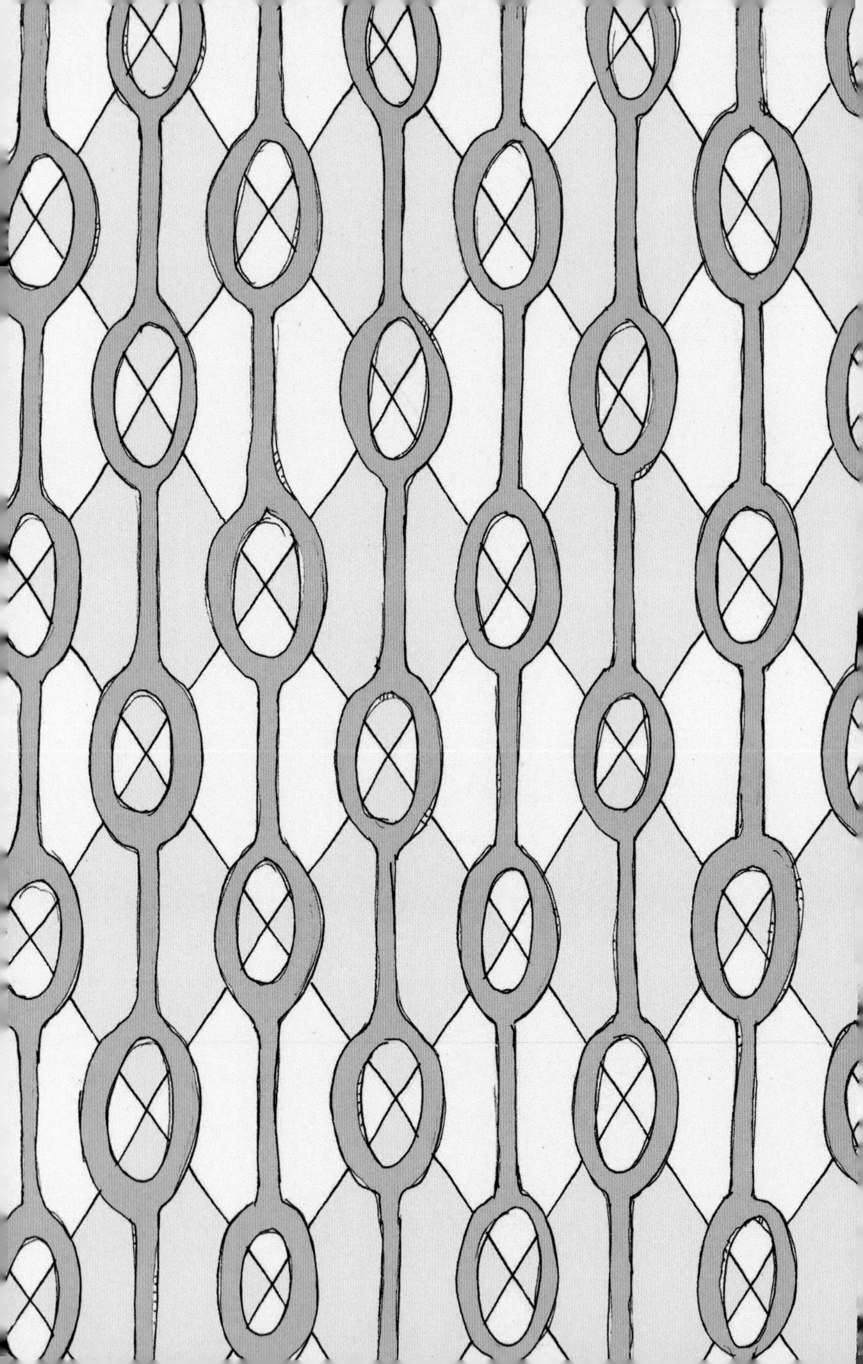

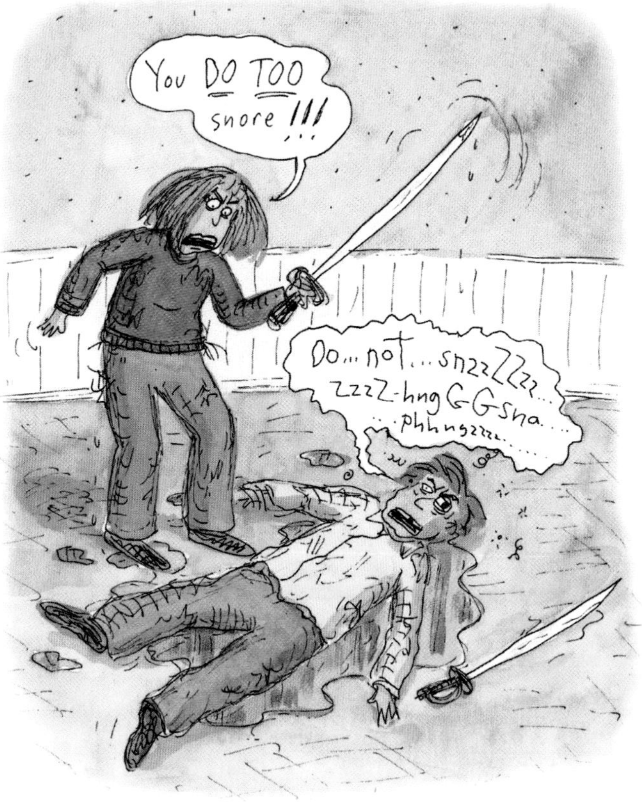
You DO TOO snore !!!
Do... not... snzzZZzz... zzzZ-hngGG-sna... ...phhngzzz...

Successful couples resolve their differences in healthy, mature ways. Like dueling.

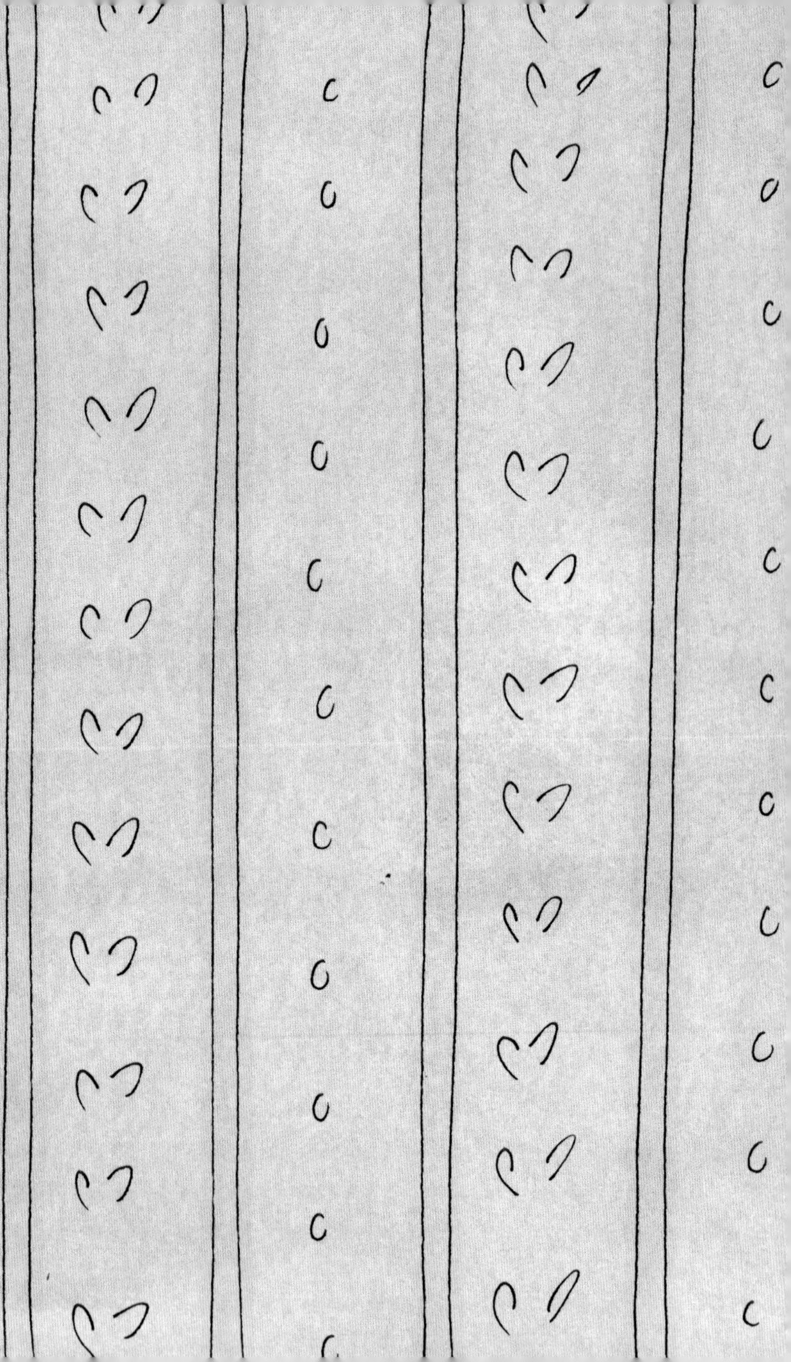

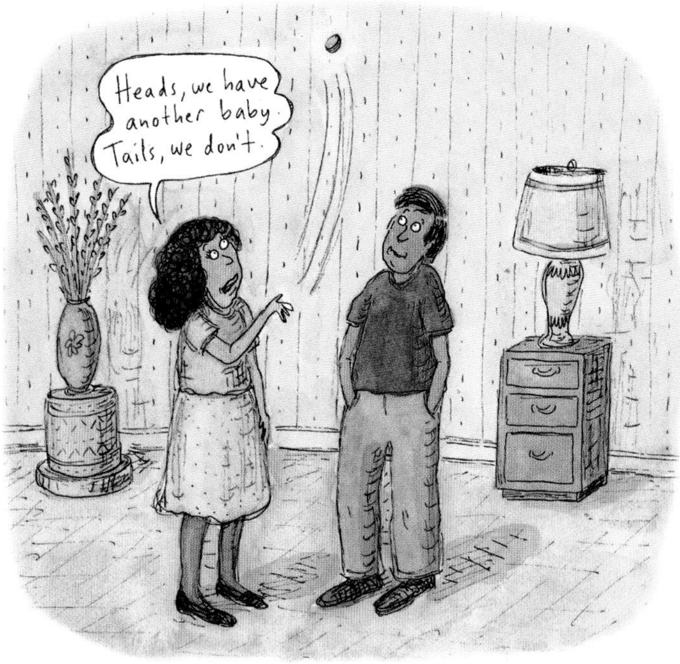
Heads, we have another baby. Tails, we don't.

Nor are they afraid to seek outside help.

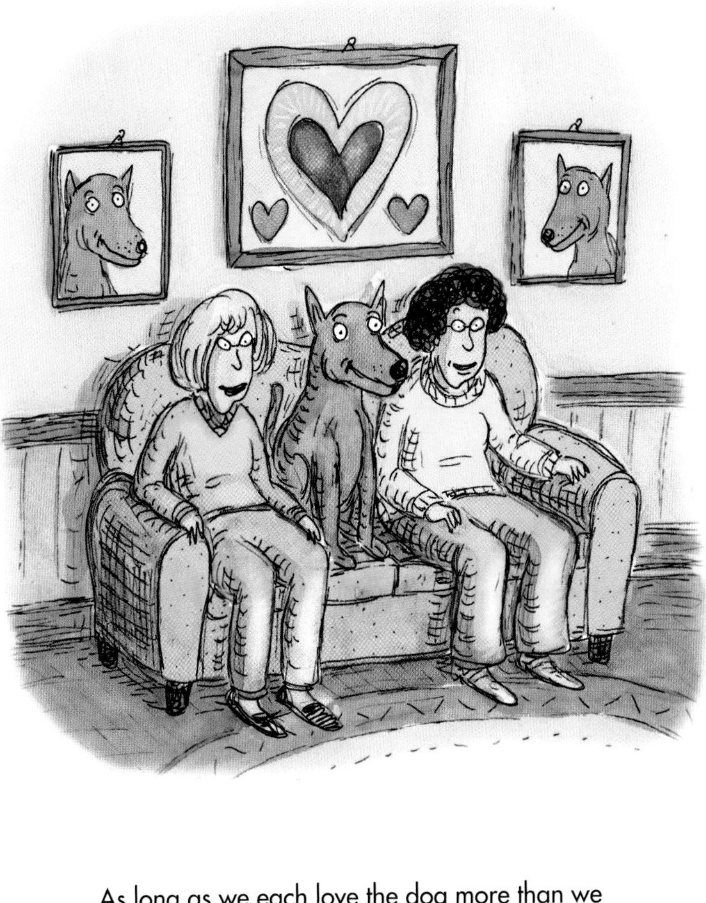

As long as we each love the dog more than we
hate each other, we will never break up.

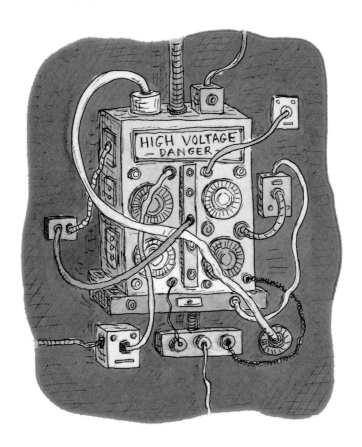

If the electricity goes out in the kitchen and
neither of us knows where the fuse box is,
it's time to move to a new house.

RINSE
FOLD
HOUSEHOLD CHORE UNIVERSITY
hereby confers upon
the degree of
WASH
DRY
DOCTOR OF LAUNDRY
KLEENO
SOFT-SO-NICE DRYER SHEETS
"QUOD SI ITA PICKY SIS, POTES FACERE"*
{*IF YOU ARE SO PICKY, YOU CAN DO IT}

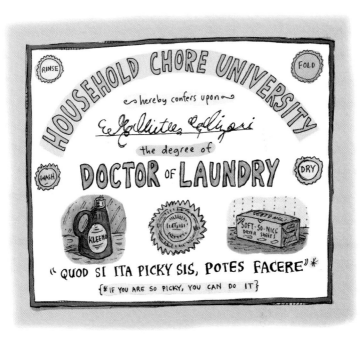

If someone is very picky about how the laundry should be done, as opposed to shoving it all in the washing machine and then shoving it all in the dryer, that someone should do the laundry.

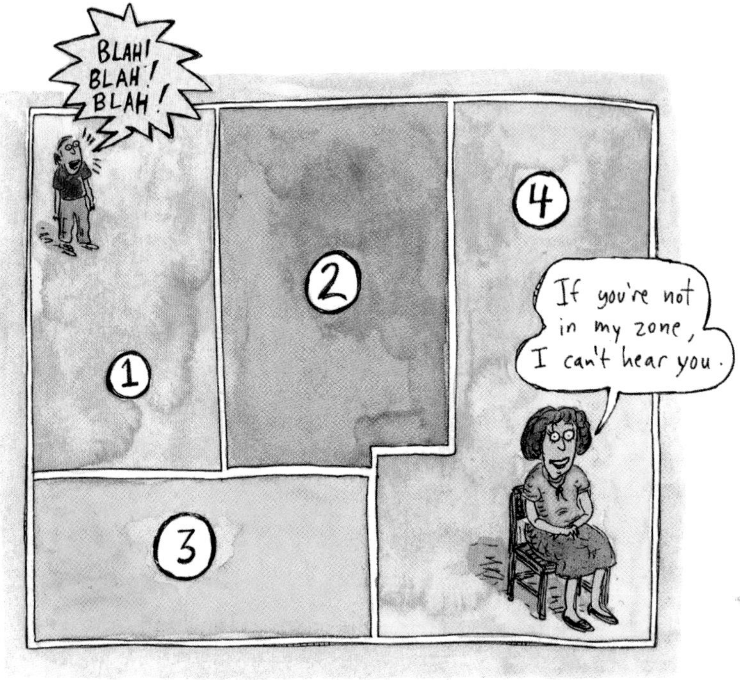
BLAH! BLAH! BLAH!
4
2
1
3
If you're not in my zone, I can't hear you.

Zoning Laws:

STEP 1: Divide house into zones.

STEP 2: No yelling from one zone to another.

STEP 3: If someone breaks this law, whisper: "You're not in my zone. I can't hear you."

STEP 4: Endlessly debate whether the hallway to the bathroom is in the same zone as the bathroom.

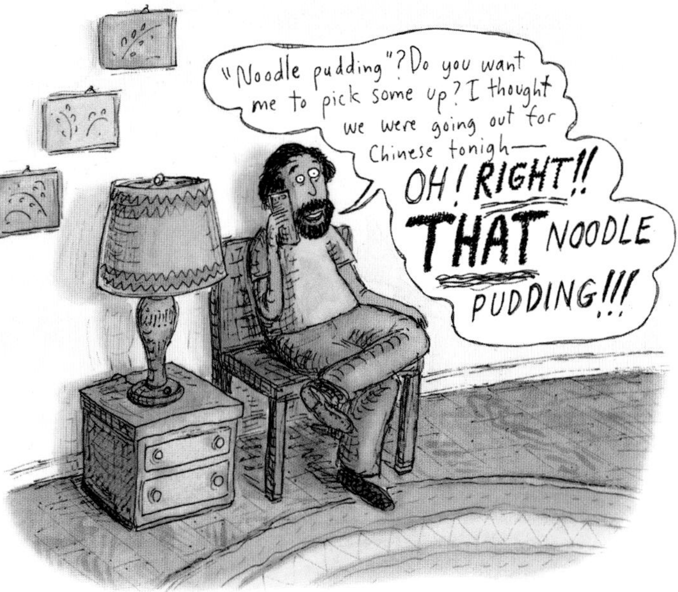
"Noodle pudding"? Do you want me to pick some up? I thought we were going out for Chinese tonigh— OH! RIGHT!! THAT NOODLE PUDDING!!!

If I'm on the phone with you and I suddenly say "noodle pudding," call the police. I'm being held at gunpoint. Or I could be hungry.

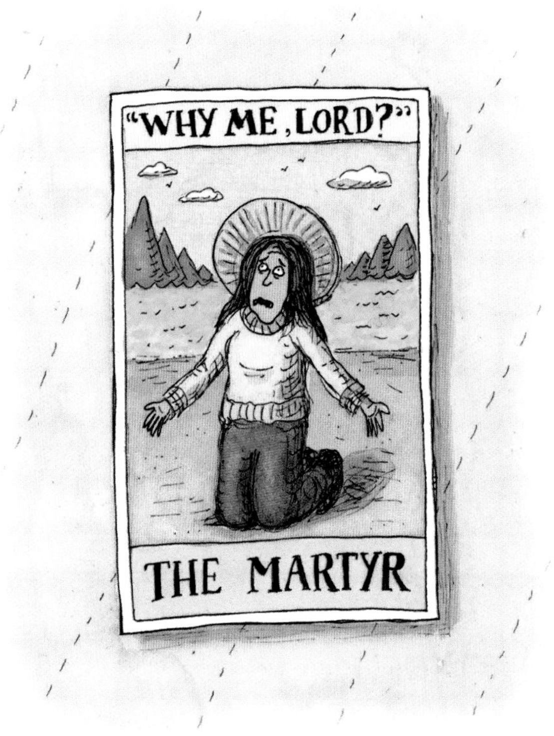
"WHY ME, LORD?"
THE MARTYR

Instead of going to your family's house down the block for Thanksgiving, magnanimously agree to travel across the country to your in-laws', where they will be serving tofurkey and Snickers salad and where you will be sleeping in the basement. Because it is always better to be the complainer than the one complained to.

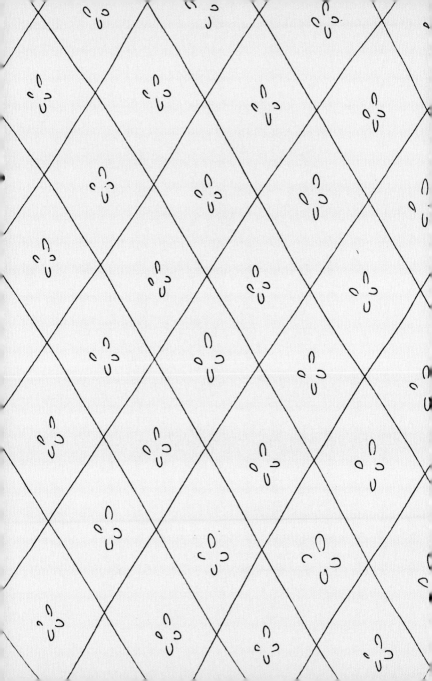

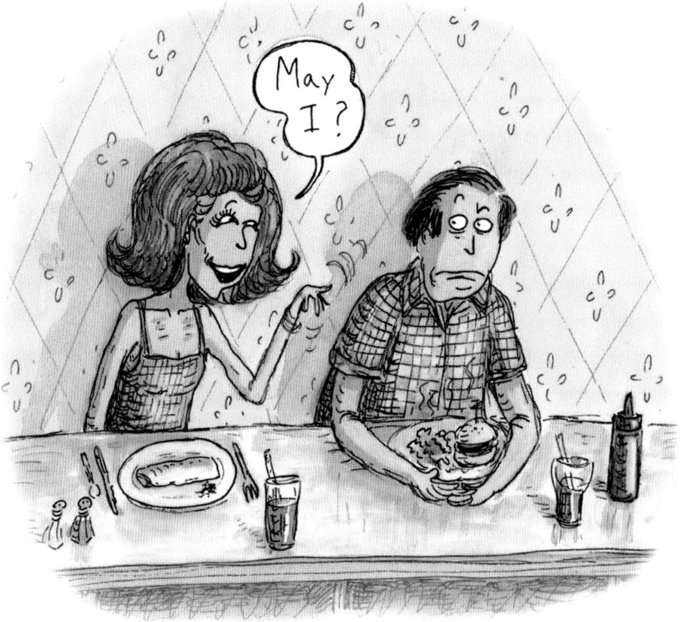
May I?

The person who ordered the egg-white omelet has to keep her skinny paws away from the other person's French fries.

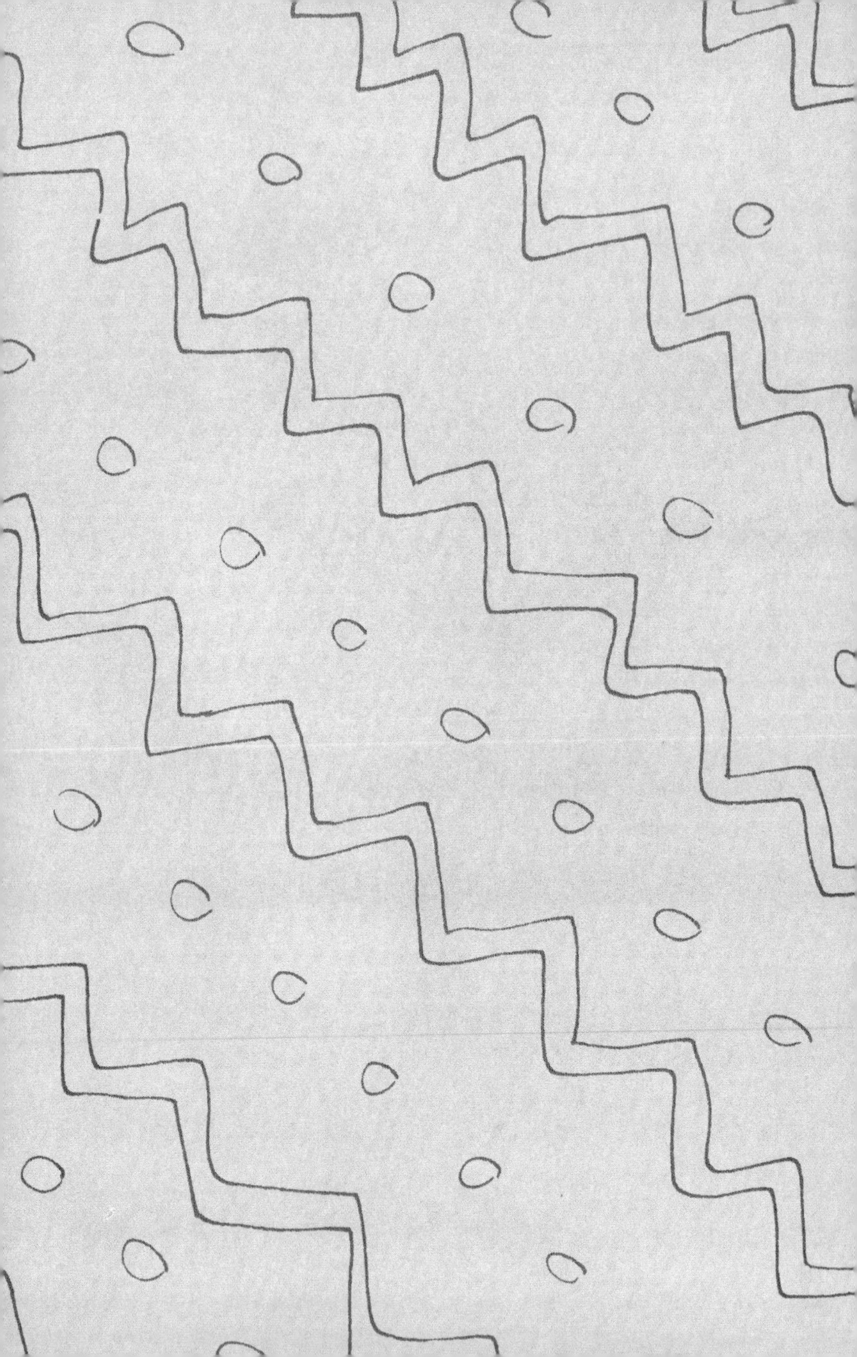

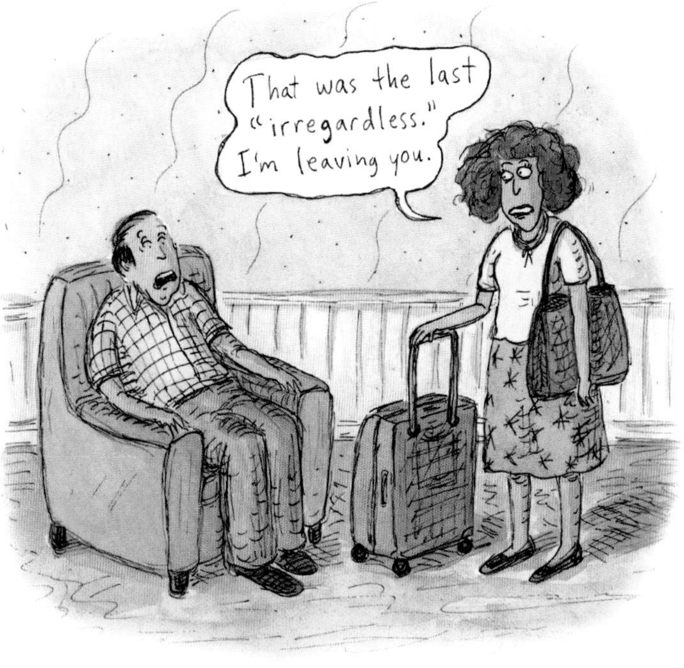
That was the last "irregardless." I'm leaving you.

If you are the Wordmeister in the relationship, don't correct the other person's every little mistake. Save it for when you cannot stand it anymore.

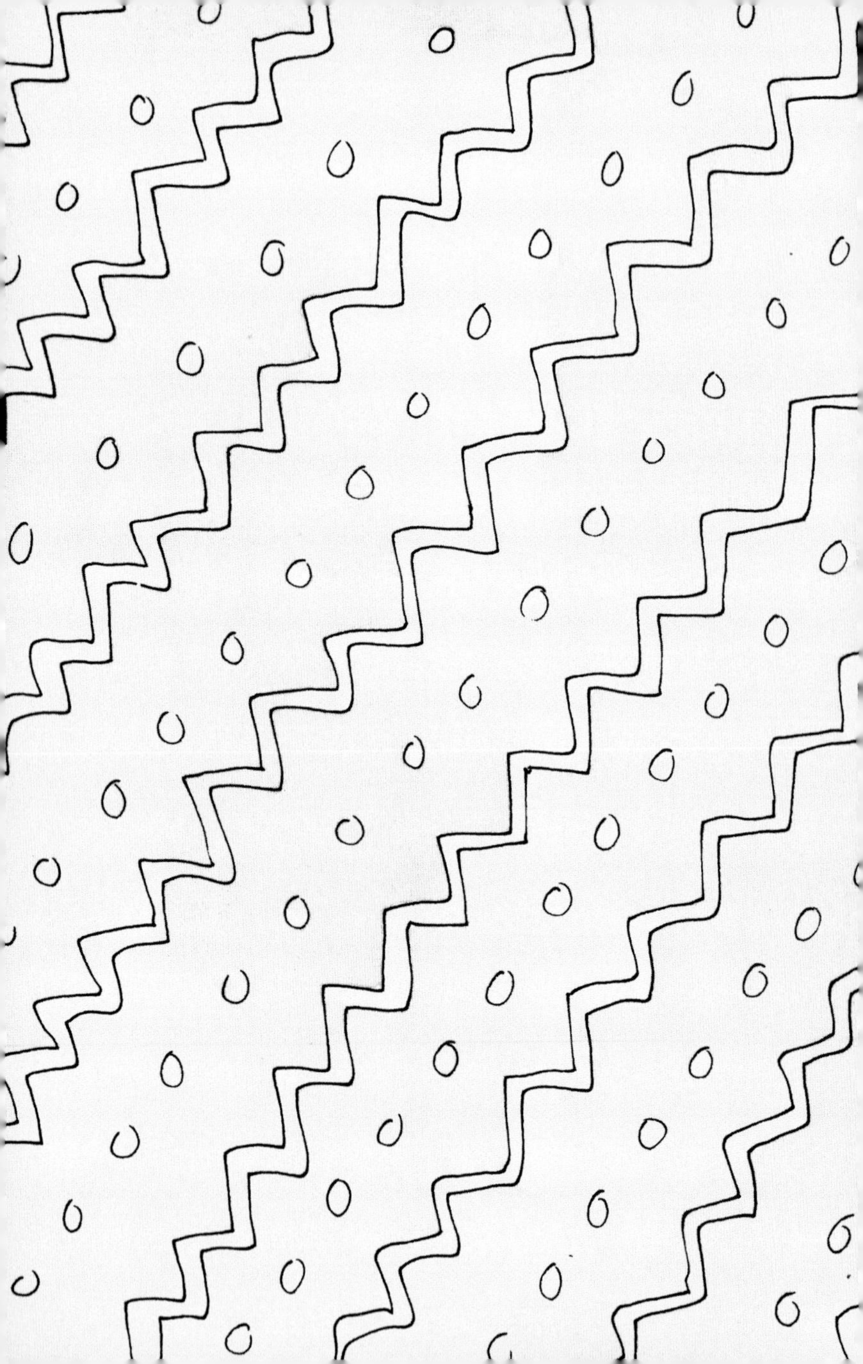

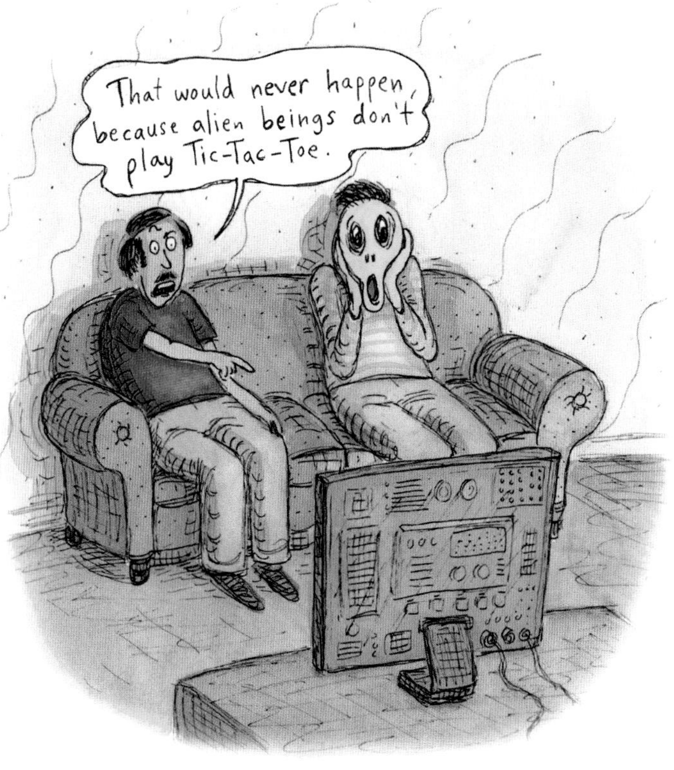
That would never happen, because alien beings don't play Tic-Tac-Toe.

No talking during TV time. If you want to rewrite the story, go in the other room.

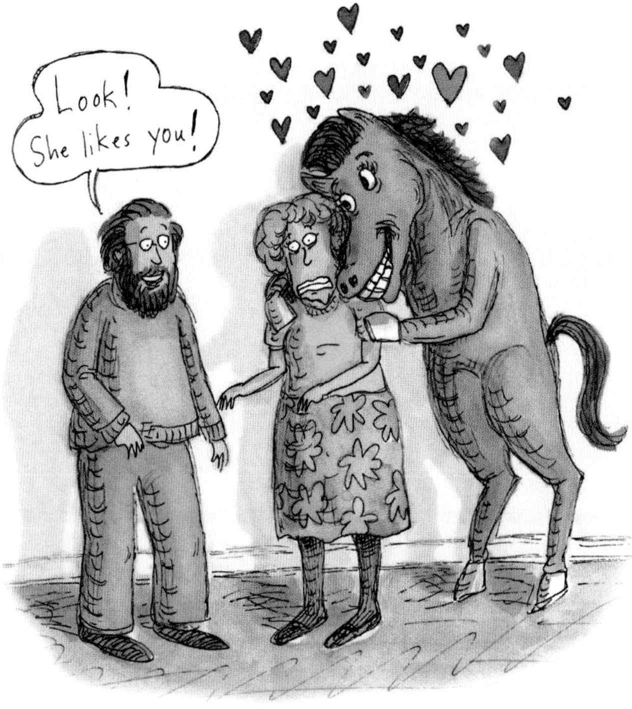
Look! She likes you!

No one should foist a pet on anyone else.

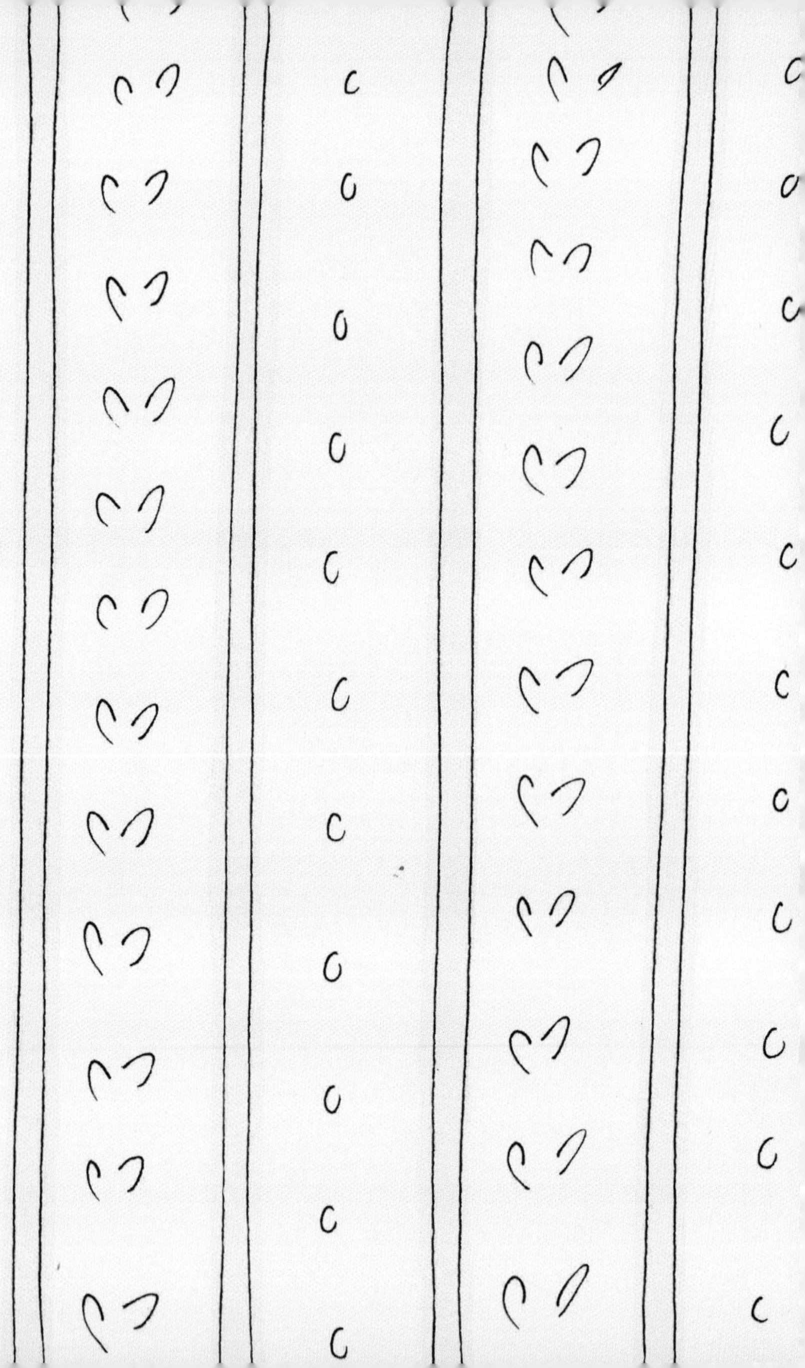

Whoever is in the state of more undress gets out of
having to pick up Olivia when she decides at 1 A.M.
that she's had enough of the slumber party.

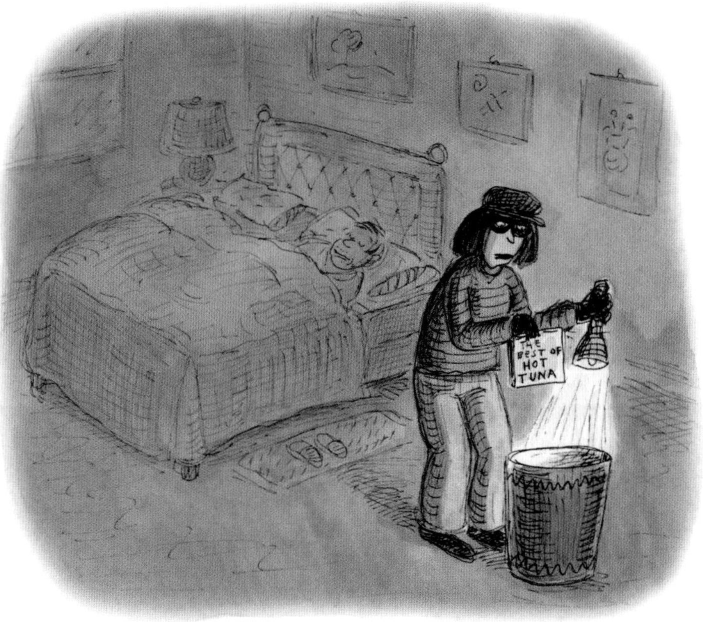
THE BEST OF HOT TUNA

Once a week, throw out something of your partner's. It will not be missed. Or noticed.

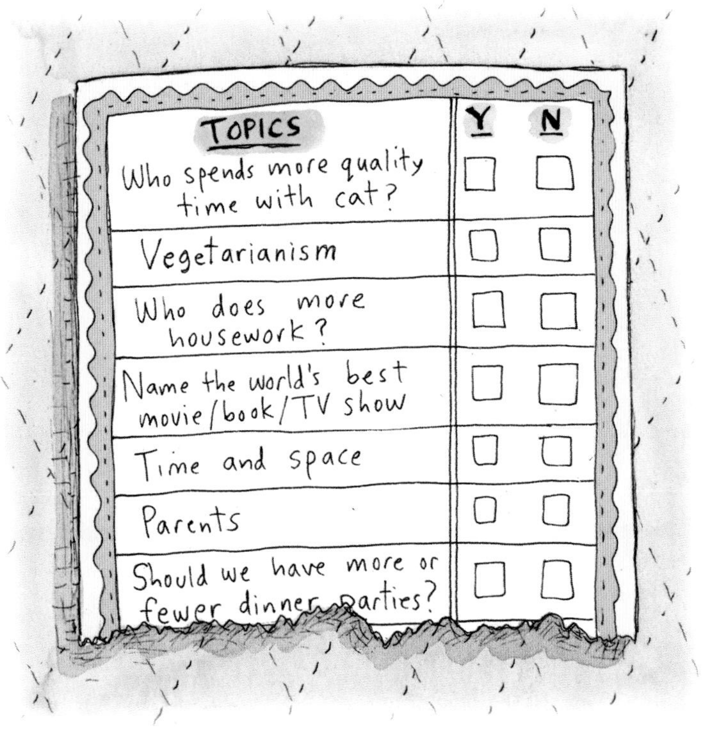
TOPICS
Y
N
Who spends more quality time with cat?
Vegetarianism
Who does more housework?
Name the world's best movie/book/TV show
Time and space
Parents
Should we have more or fewer dinner parties?

Before setting out on a long road trip,
agree on what to fight about in the car.

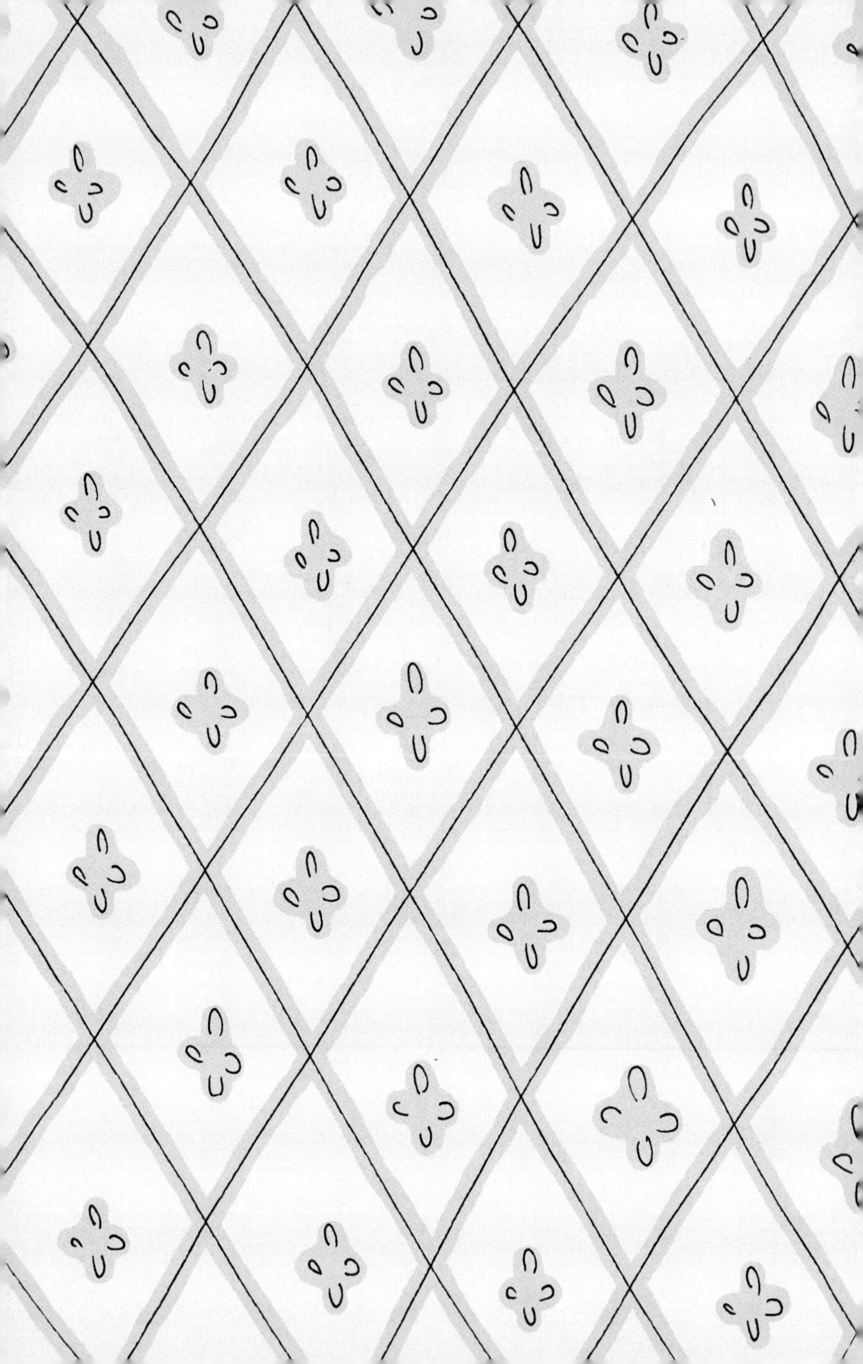

You get to kvetch for three minutes and then
your time is up, unless you are in a Chekhov play,
in which case you have two hours.

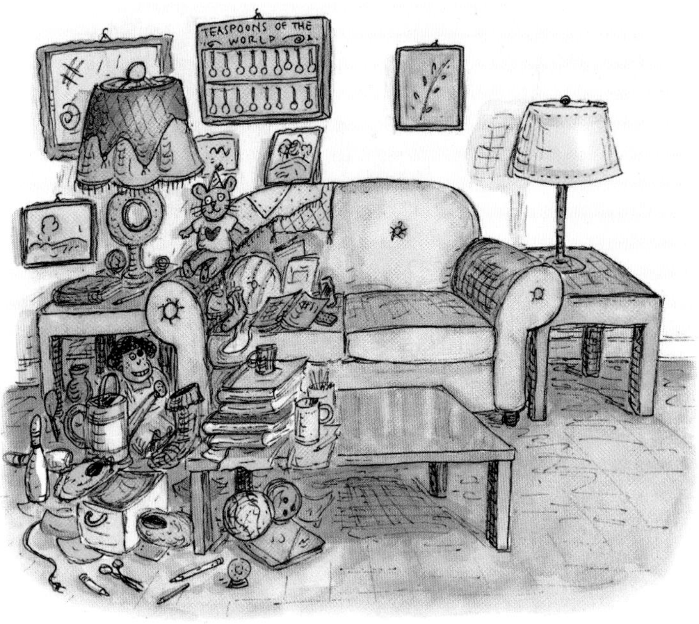
TEASPOONS OF THE WORLD

Do not let your housemate's clutter proliferate into your shared territory. Remember how the appeasement policy of the Allies led to Hitler's invasion of Poland? That's what will happen to the living room.

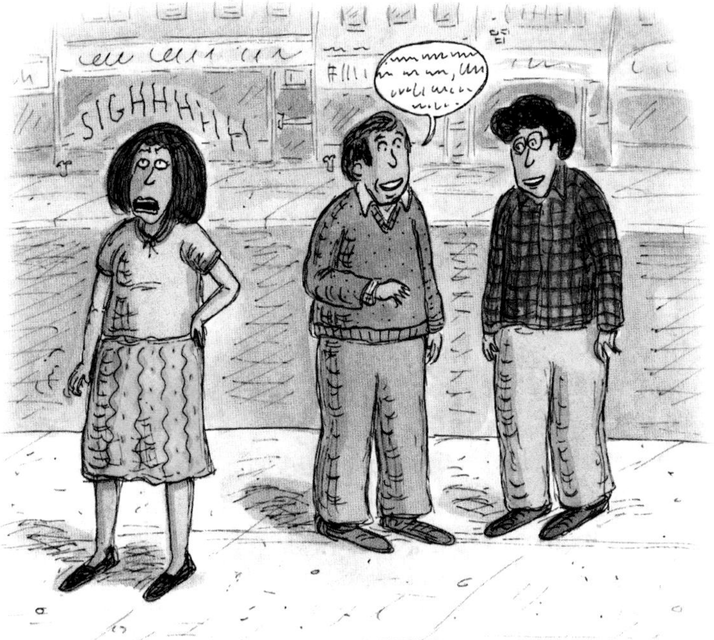
SIGHHHHH

If I tell a story you've heard before, don't roll your eyes and say to the Lippmans, "I wonder how it'll turn out this time!" or "I'd rather swim in the toilet than listen to this again."

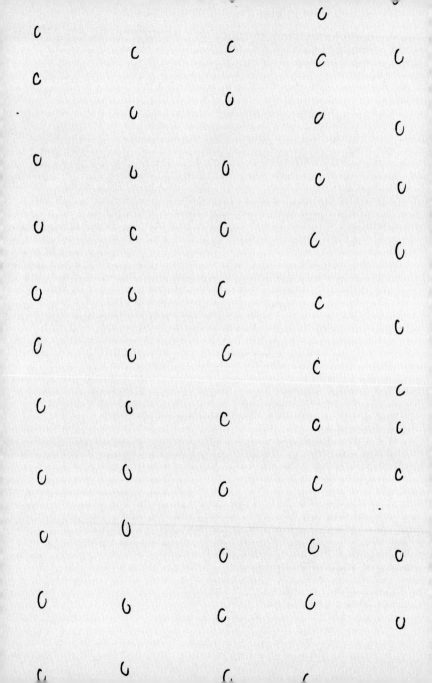

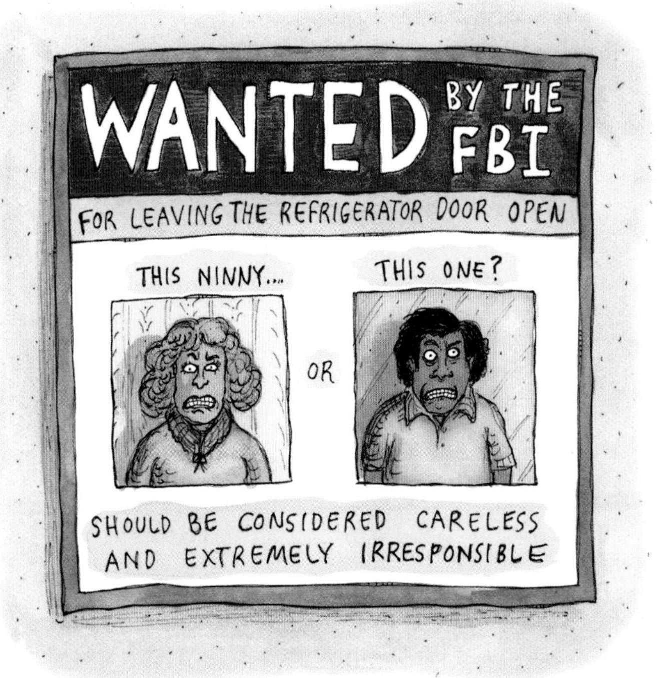
WANTED BY THE FBI
FOR LEAVING THE REFRIGERATOR DOOR OPEN
THIS NINNY...
OR
THIS ONE?
SHOULD BE CONSIDERED CARELESS
AND EXTREMELY IRRESPONSIBLE

Stop bickering about which one of you
left the refrigerator door open last night.
Call in the FBI to do an investigation.

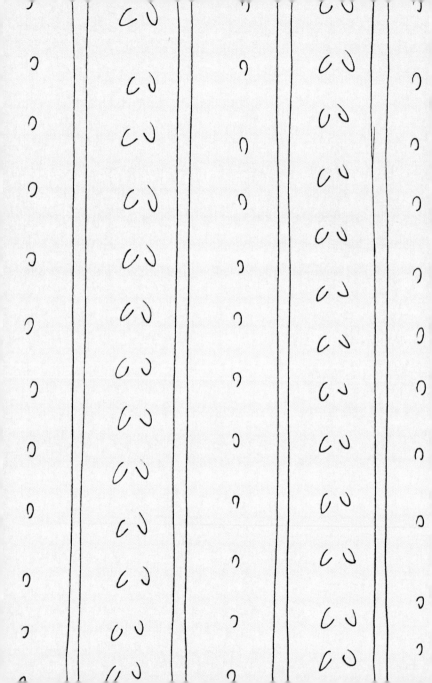

Never go to a couples' counselor who says,
"How would you feel if I told you I was
in love with your partner?"

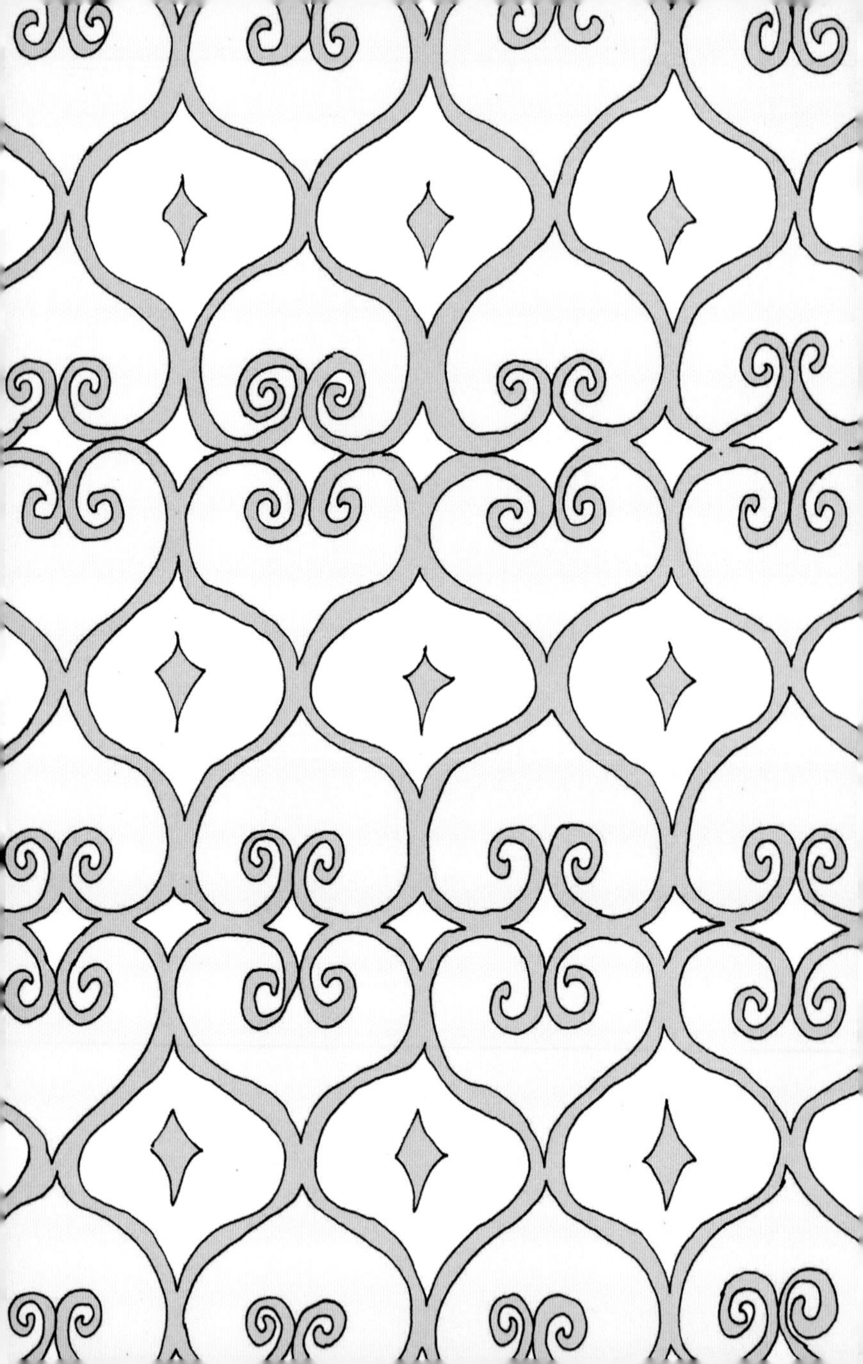

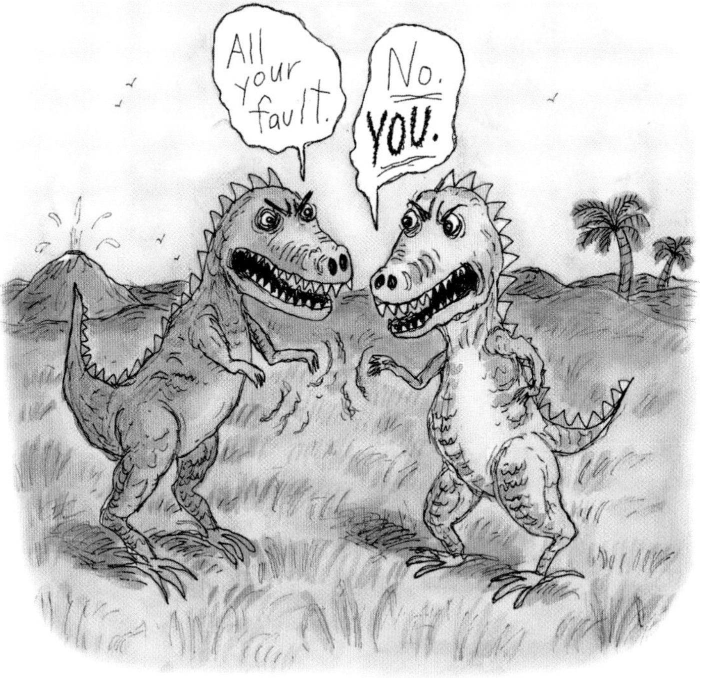
All your fault.
No. YOU.

If you are fighting, it means you are still together.

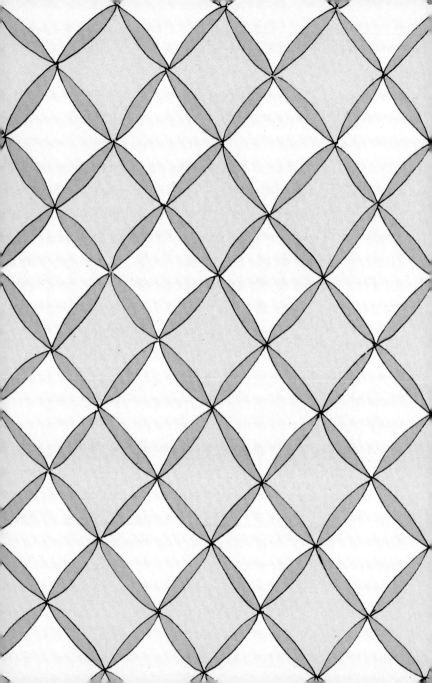

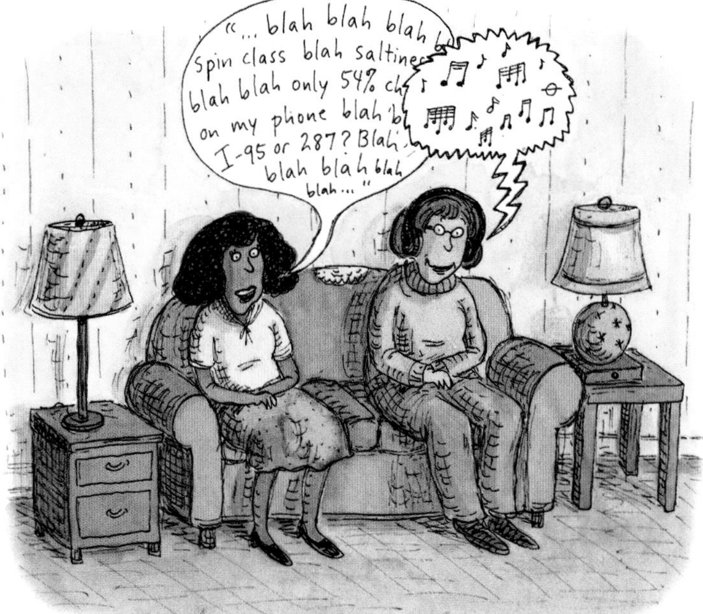
"... blah blah blah Spin class blah saltine blah blah only 54% ch on my phone blah I-95 or 287? Blah blah blah blah blah ..."

Earphones.

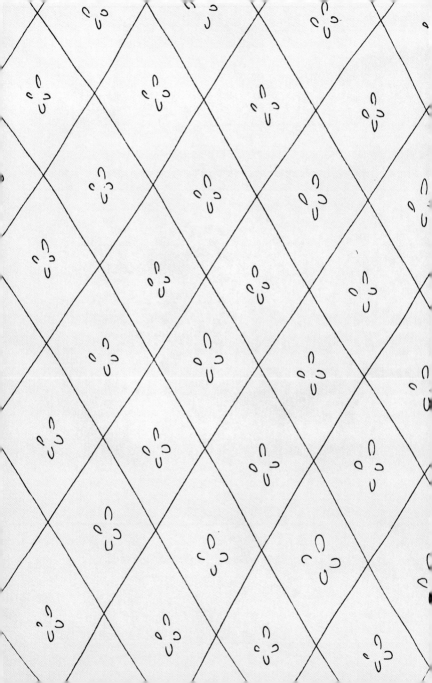

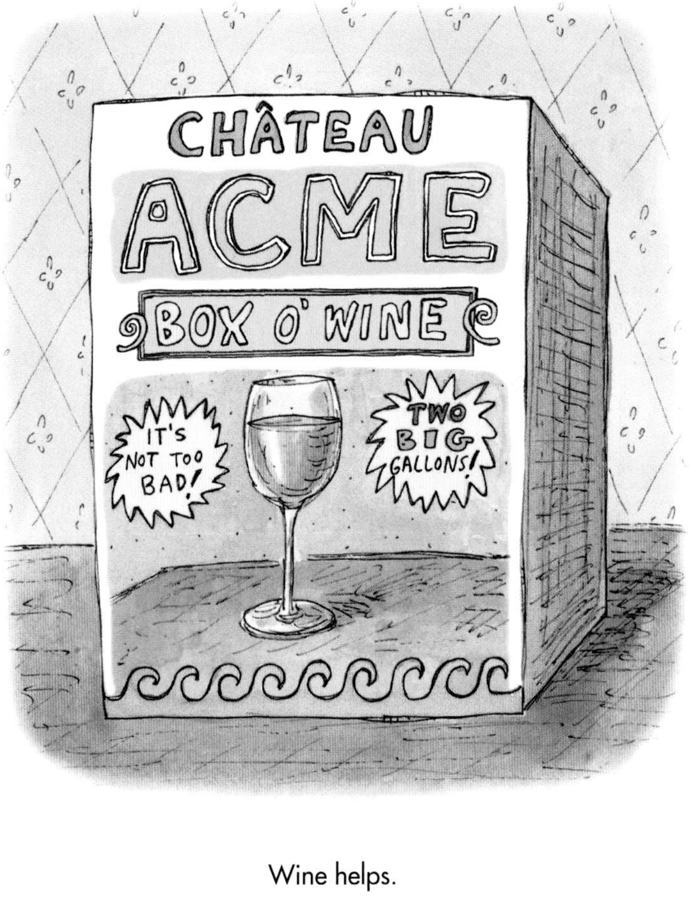
CHÂTEAU
ACME
BOX O' WINE
IT'S NOT TOO BAD!
TWO BIG GALLONS!

Wine helps.

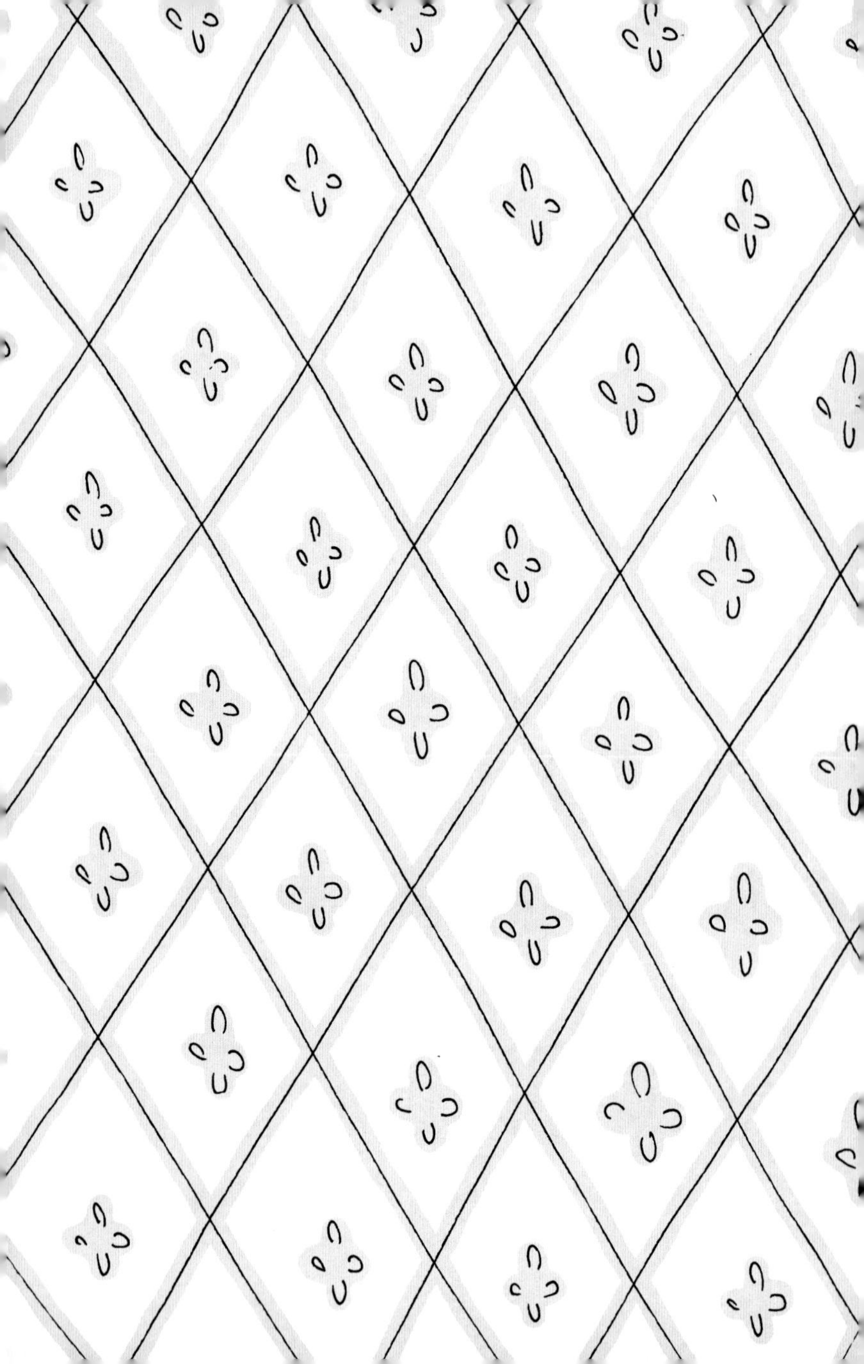

Whoever cares the most that there are crumbs
in the toaster gets the de-crumbing job.

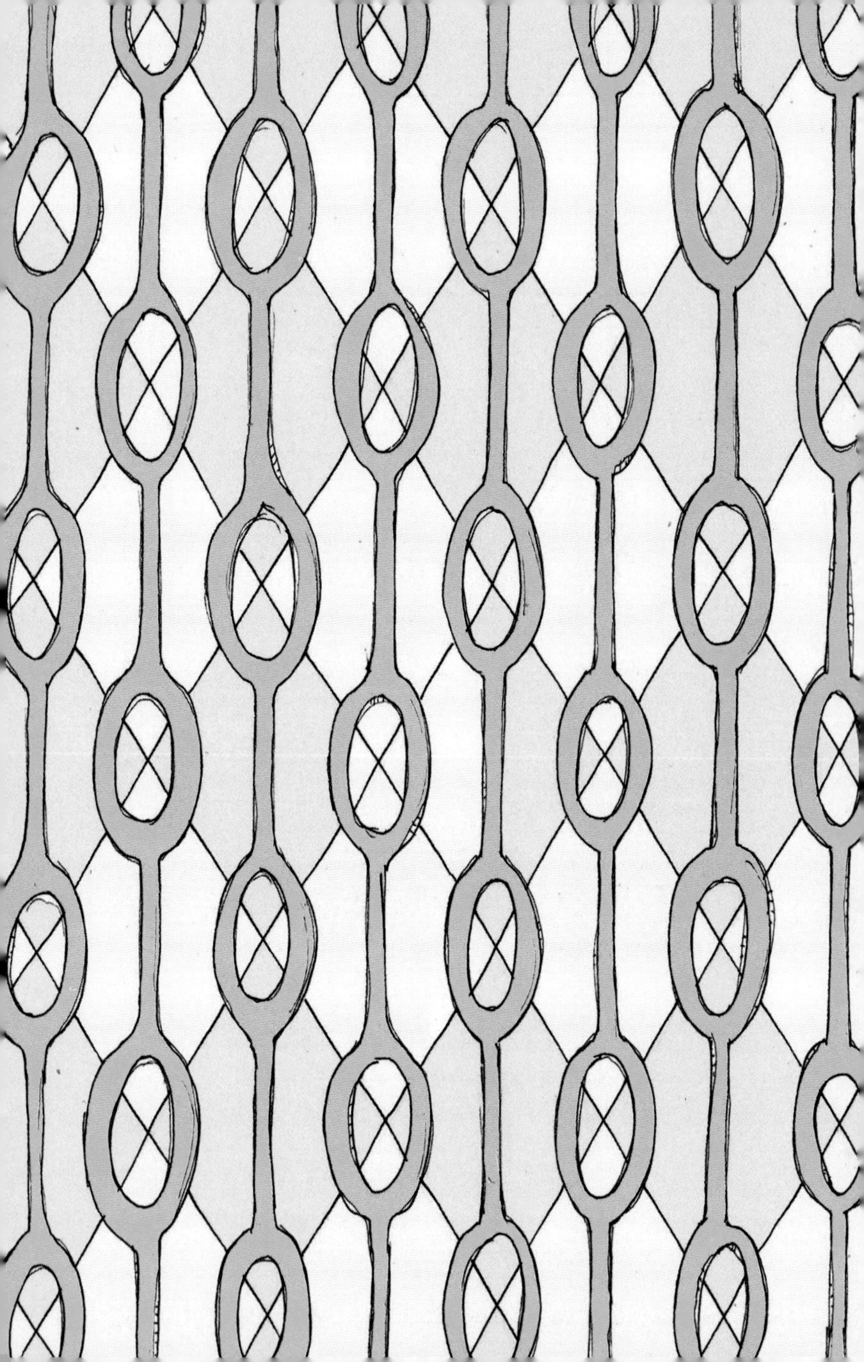

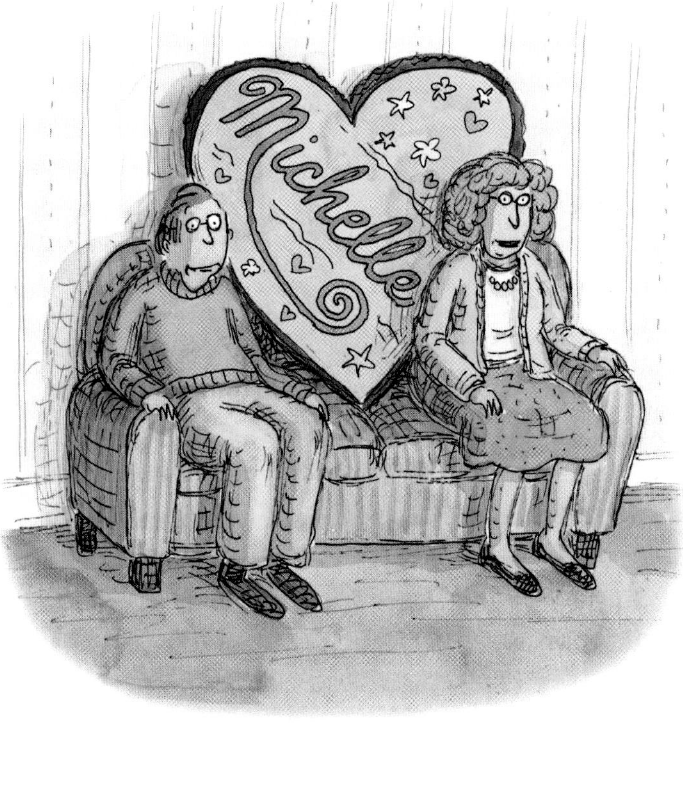
Michelle

If either of you has a chance
with Michelle Obama, go for it.

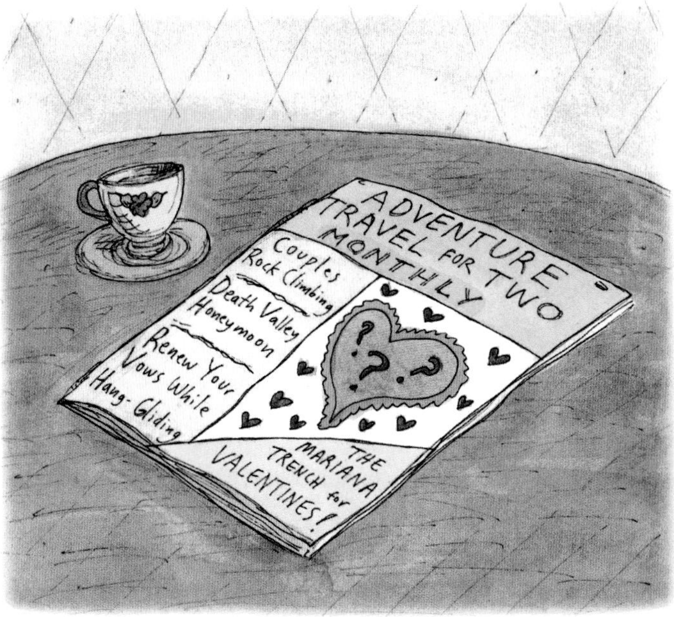
ADVENTURE TRAVEL FOR TWO MONTHLY
Couples Rock Climbing
Death Valley Honeymoon
Renew Your Vows While Hang-Gliding
THE MARIANA TRENCH for VALENTINES!

Don't kayak in rough waters with the beneficiary of your life insurance policy.

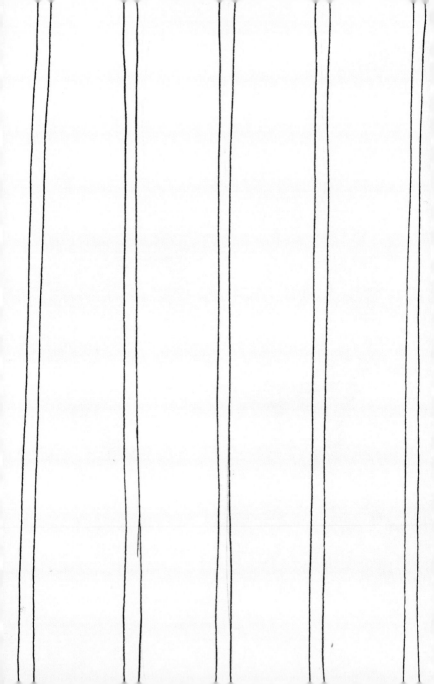

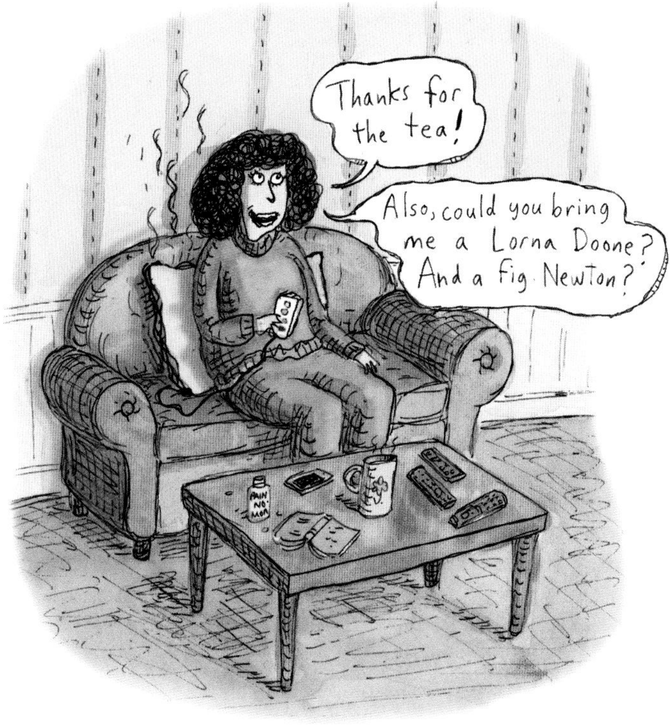
Thanks for the tea!
Also, could you bring me a Lorna Doone? And a Fig Newton?

It is less stressful to fall off a ladder and pull a muscle in your back than to convince someone to steady the ladder because no, you're not neurotic for thinking ceiling fans need to be cleaned even if nobody sees the dirty part.

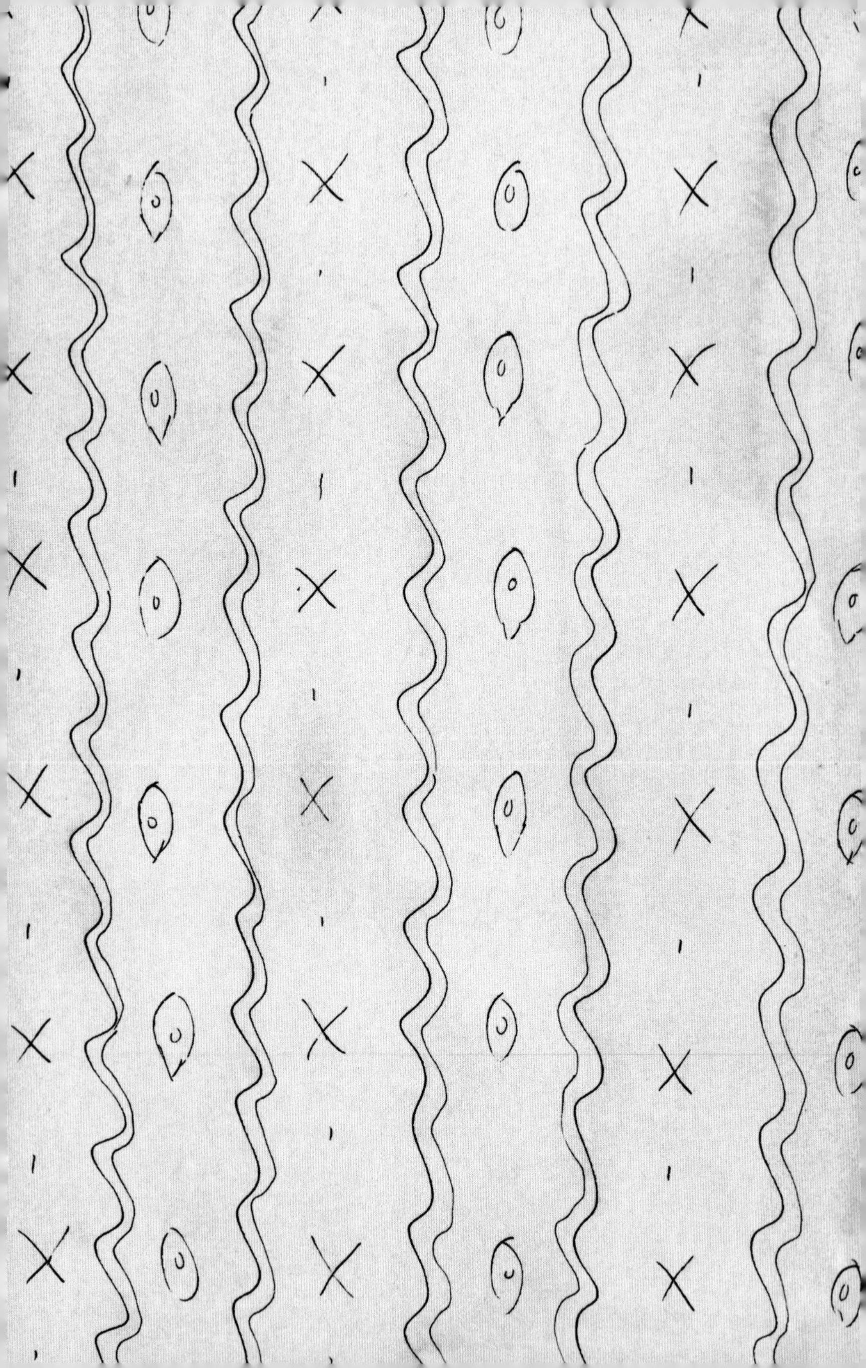

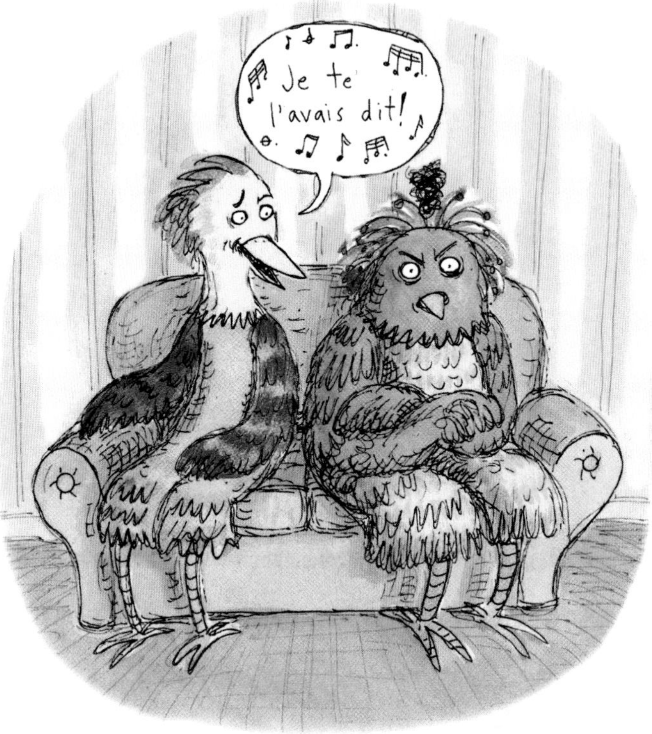
Je te l'avais dit!

If you feel an urge to say, "I told you so,"
say it in French.

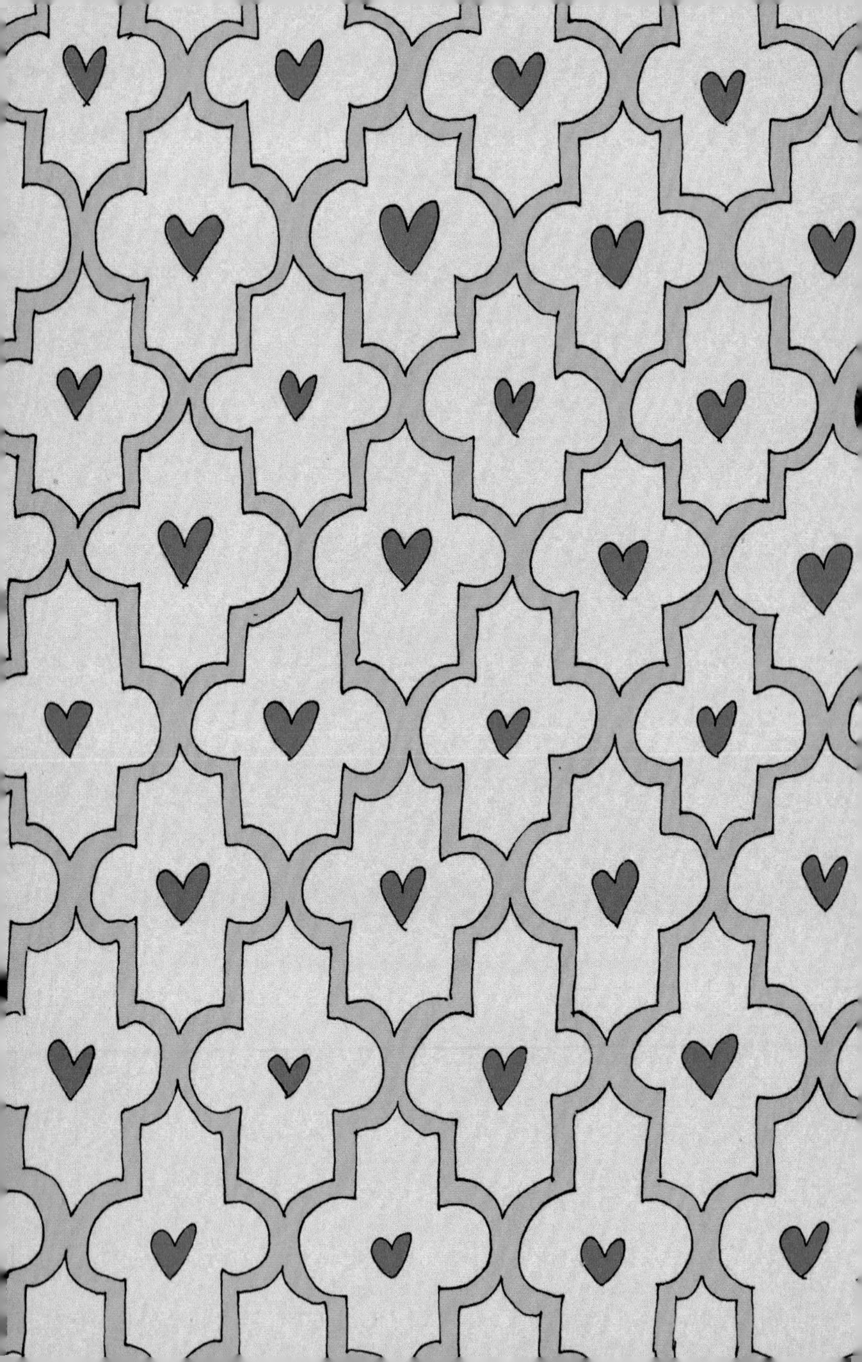

Marriage is one of you secretly turning the
thermostat up and the other secretly turning it down
and so on and so on until one of you dies.

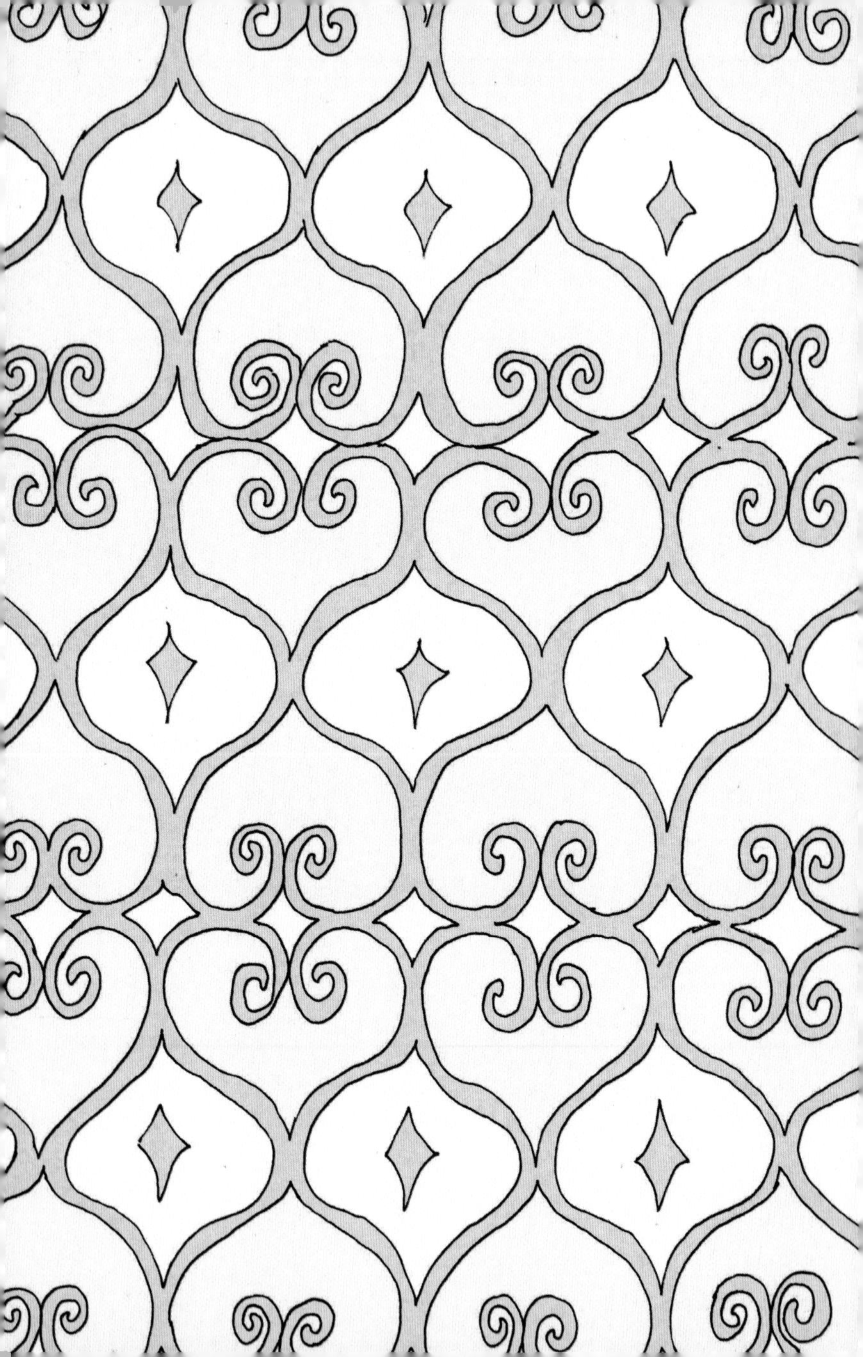

The wrong answer is better than no answer.

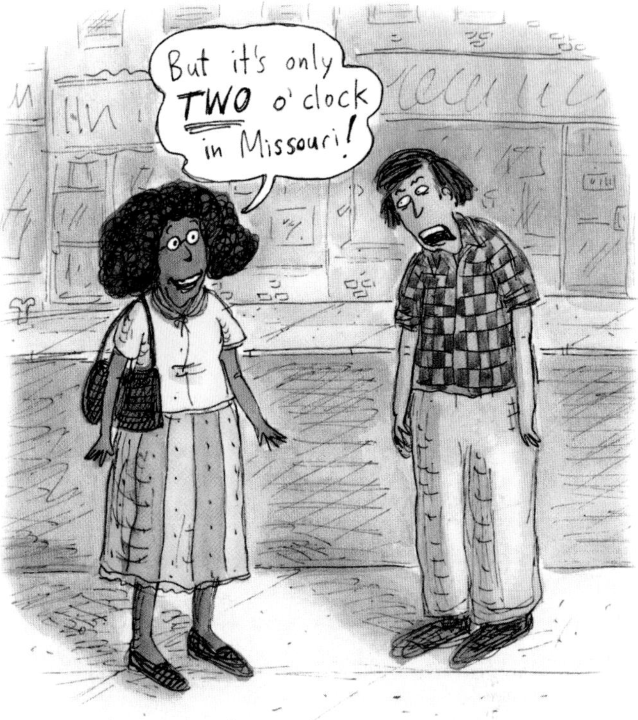
But it's only TWO o' clock in Missouri!

You are allowed to be late twice. After that, if the relationship is to survive, you must move westward to another time zone.

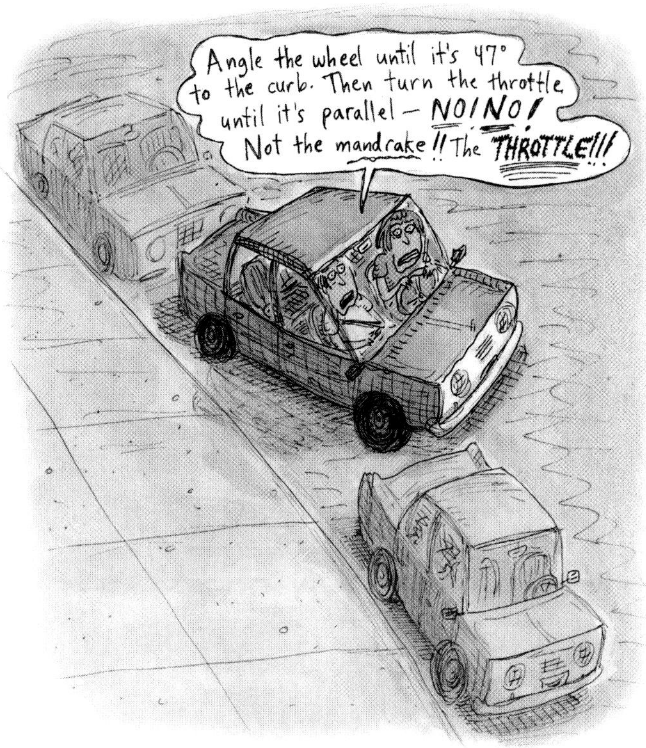
Angle the wheel until it's 47° to the curb. Then turn the throttle until it's parallel — NO! NO! Not the mandrake!! The THROTTLE!!!

Trying to park with your spouse in the car
is like brushing your teeth in front
of the dental hygienist.

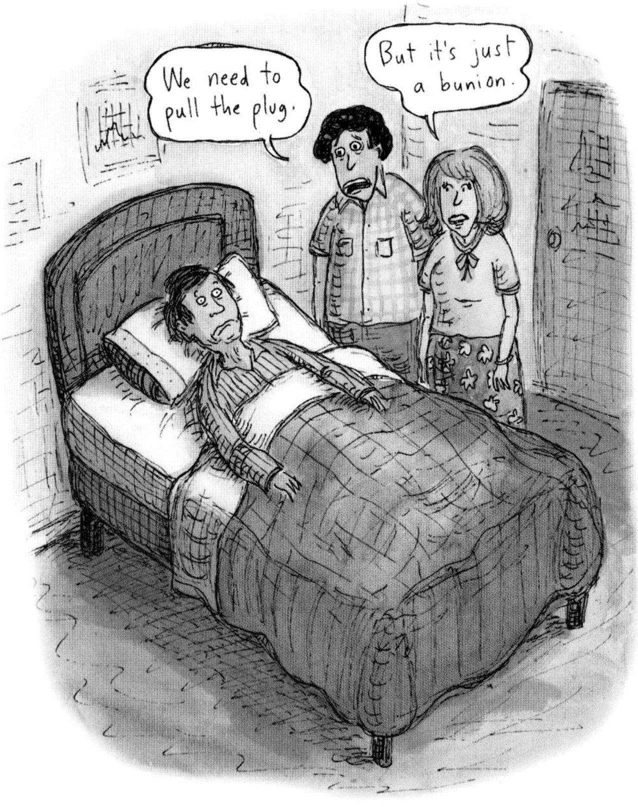
We need to pull the plug.
But it's just a bunion.

It's more fun being the pessimist than the optimist, so take turns.

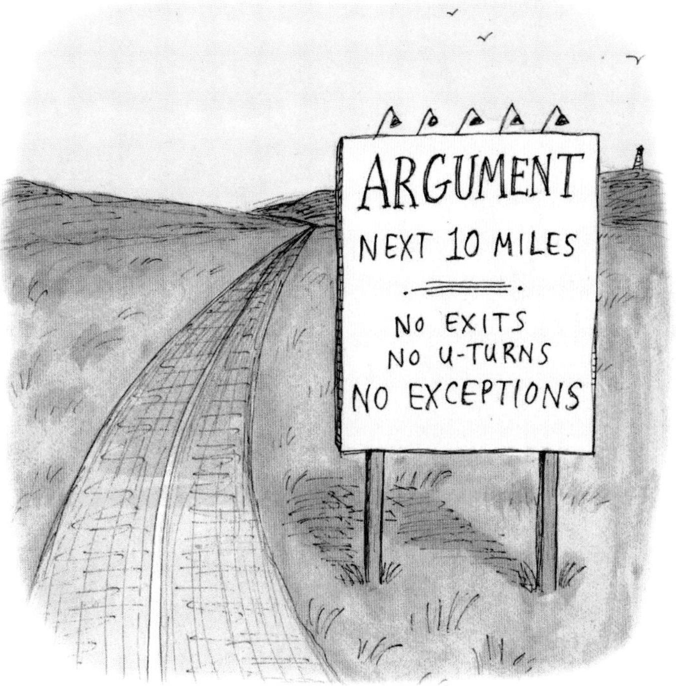
ARGUMENT
NEXT 10 MILES
NO EXITS
NO U-TURNS
NO EXCEPTIONS

If you are in the middle of an argument
and realize, after going way out on a limb,
that you are wrong, do not turn back.

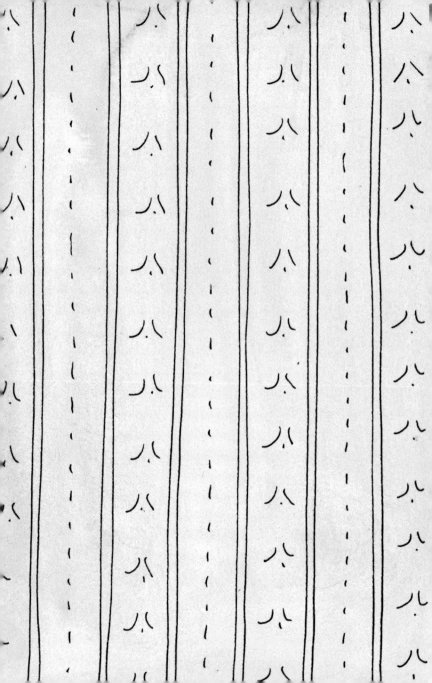

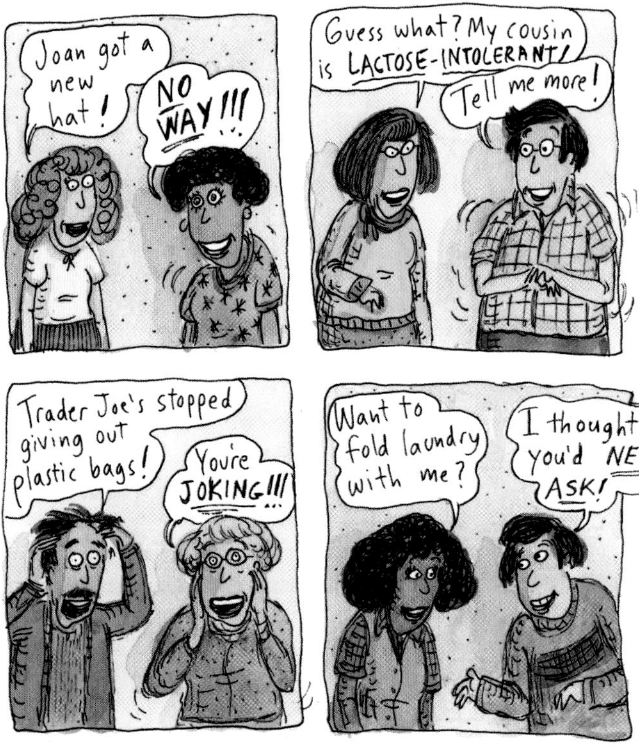
Joan got a new hat!
NO WAY!!!
Guess what? My cousin is LACTOSE-INTOLERANT!
Tell me more!
Trader Joe's stopped giving out plastic bags!
You're JOKING!!!
Want to fold laundry with me?
I thought you'd NEVER ASK!

Happy couples find the same boring things fascinating.

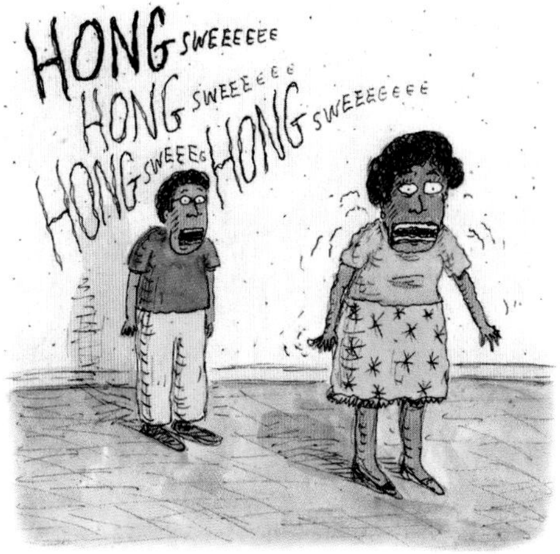
HONG SWEEEEEE
HONG SWEEEEEE
HONG SWEEEE HONG SWEEEEEEEE

If you must breathe, don't breathe so loudly.

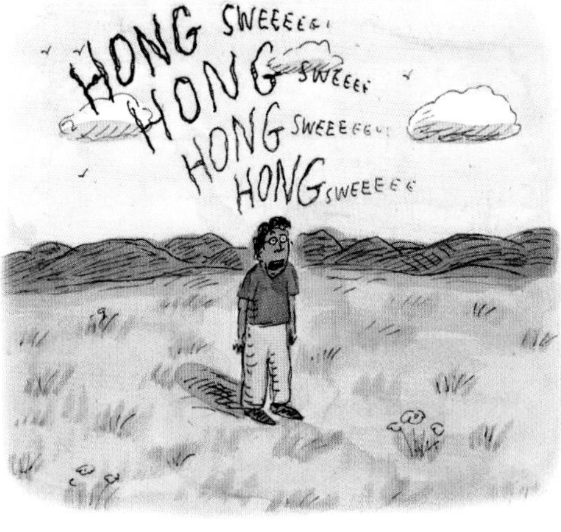
HONG SWEEEEE
HONG SWEEEE
HONG SWEEEEE
HONG SWEEEEE

If you must breathe so loudly, do it outside.

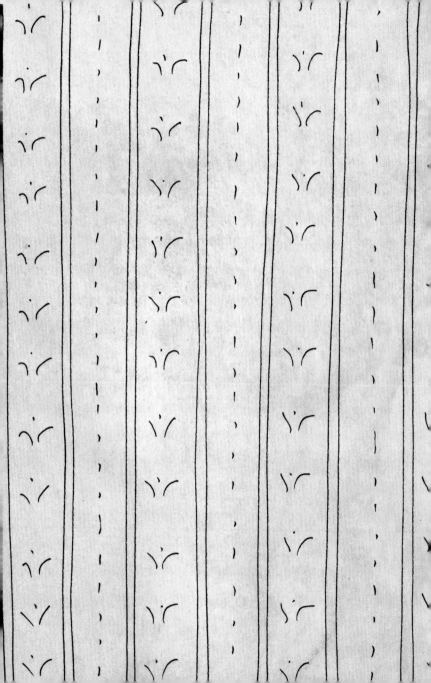

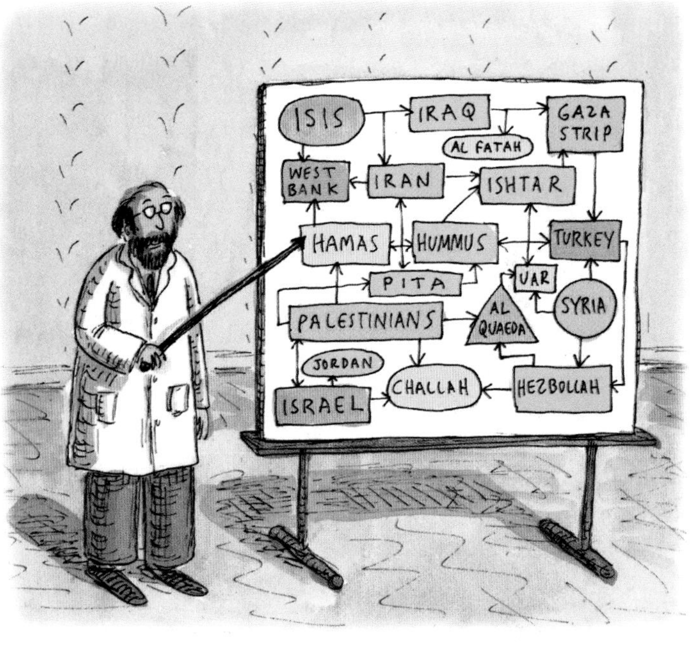
ISIS
IRAQ
GAZA STRIP
AL FATAH
WEST BANK
IRAN
ISHTAR
HAMAS
HUMMUS
TURKEY
PITA
UAR
AL QUAEDA
SYRIA
PALESTINIANS
JORDAN
ISRAEL
CHALLAH
HEZBOLLAH

No need for both of you to follow current events in the Middle East. One of you handle that and the other can keep track of where the TV remote is.

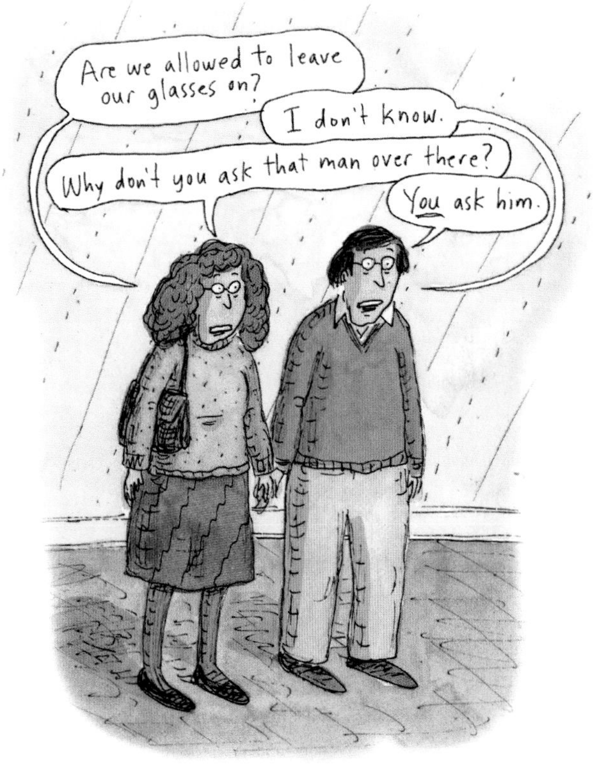
Are we allowed to leave our glasses on?
I don't know.
Why don't you ask that man over there?
You ask him.

Never go to orgies alone.

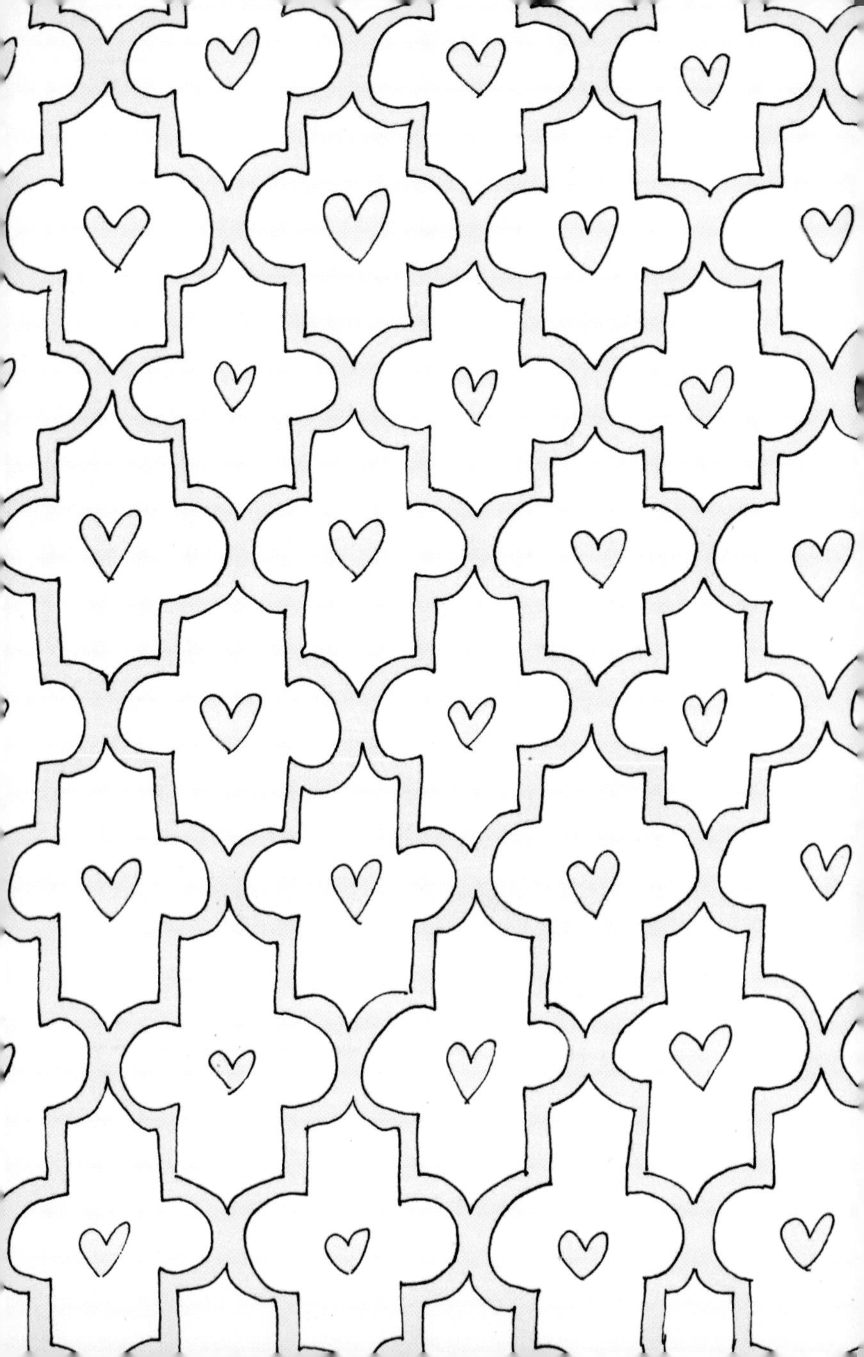

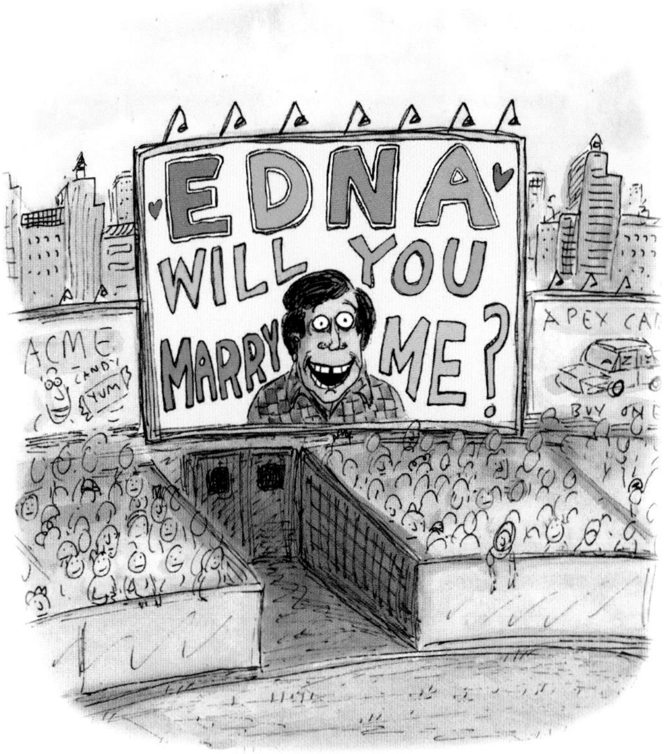
EDNA
WILL YOU
MARRY ME?
ACME
CANDY
YUM
APEX CA
BUY ON

Never say yes to someone who proposes marriage
on a stadium jumbotron.

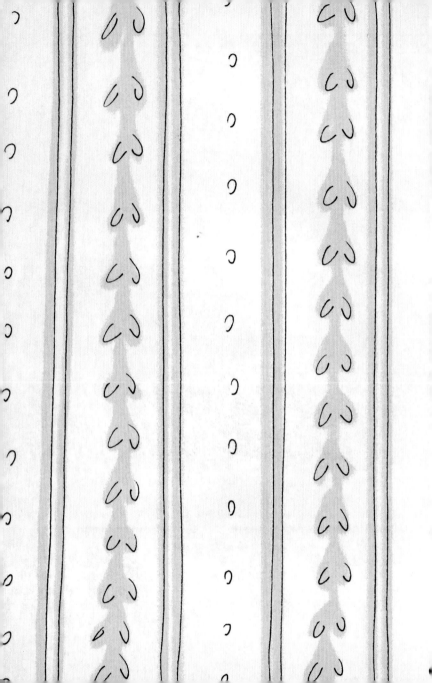

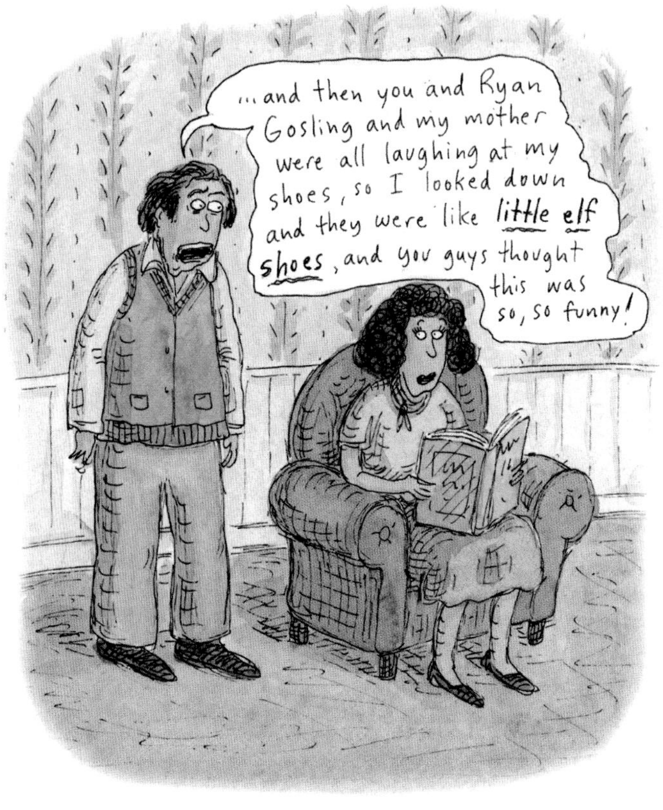
...and then you and Ryan Gosling and my mother were all laughing at my shoes, so I looked down and they were like little elf shoes, and you guys thought this was so, so funny!

You can't break up with someone for something they did in your dream.

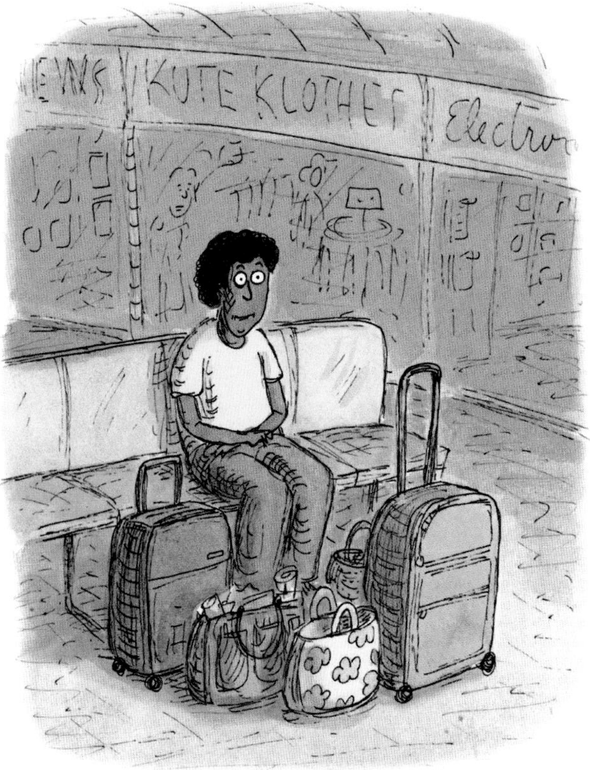
KUTE KLOTHES

Remember: if you were single, there'd be nobody to watch your luggage in the airport while you go to the restroom.

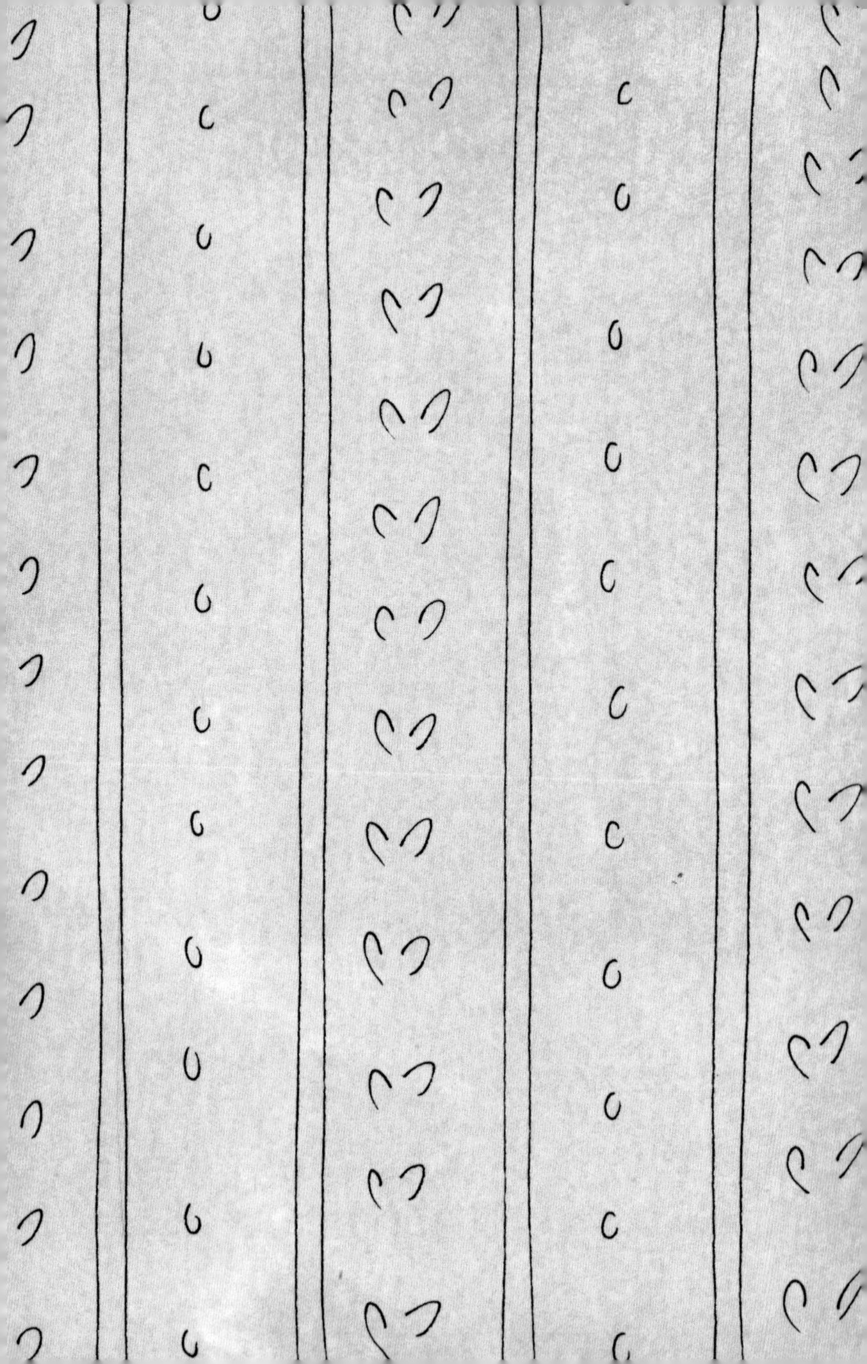

Or check you for ticks.

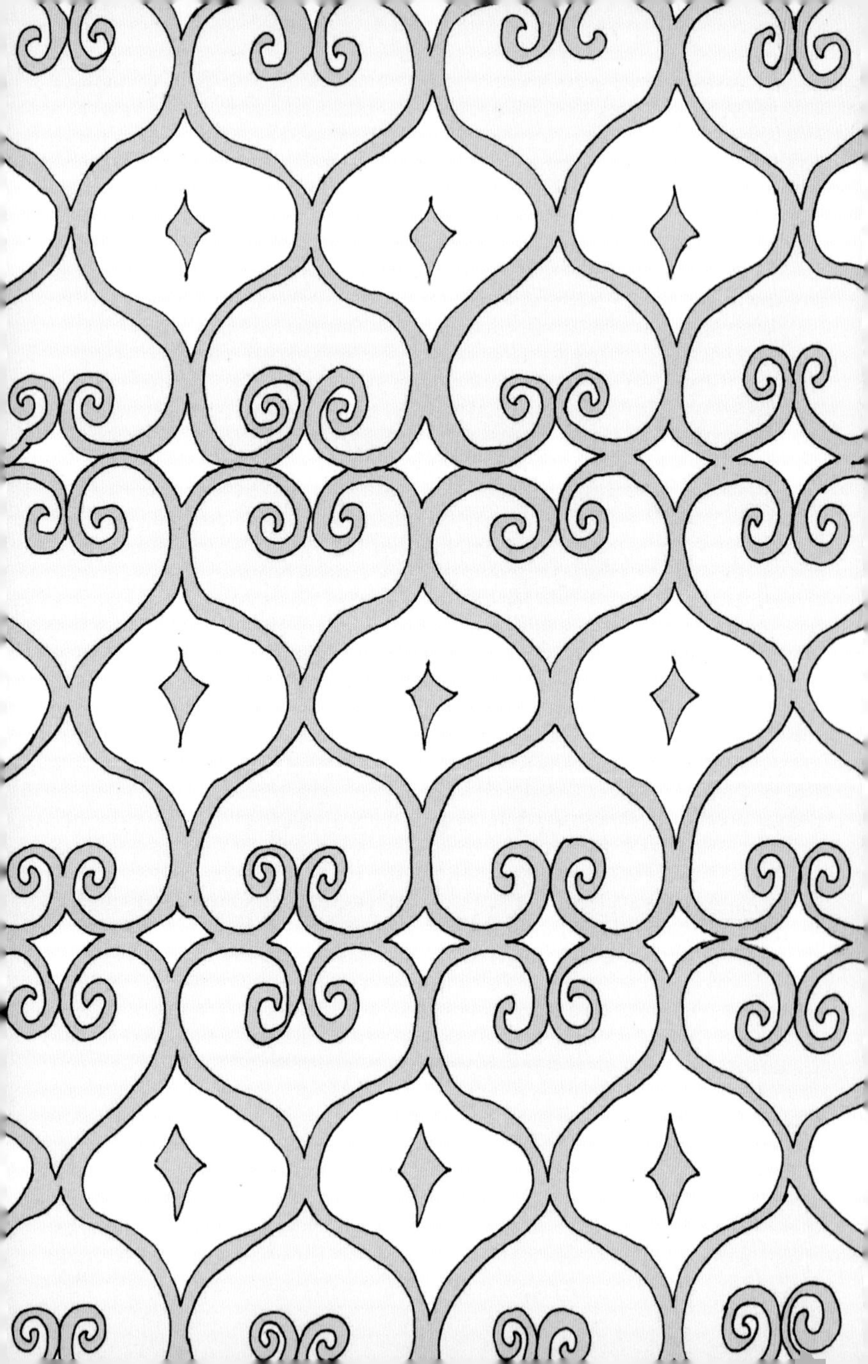

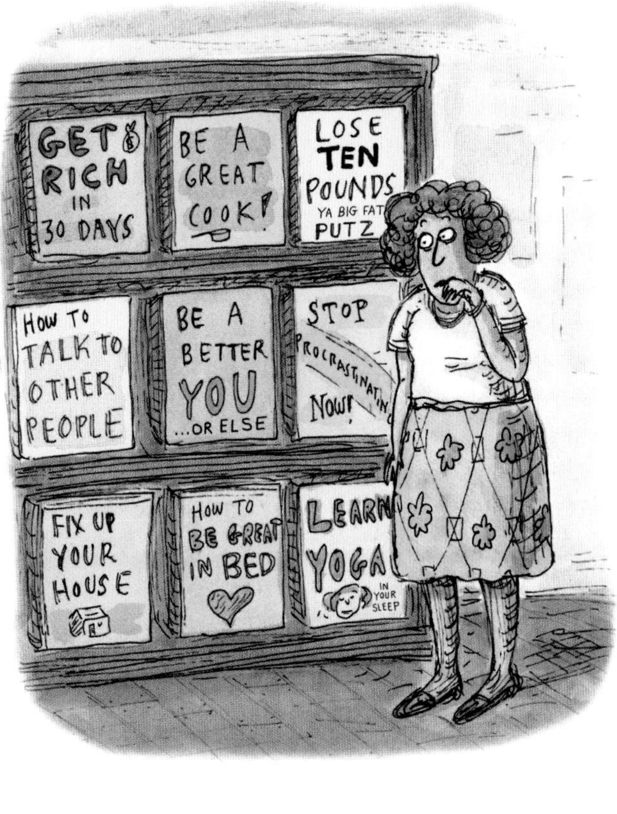
GET RICH IN 30 DAYS
BE A GREAT COOK!
LOSE TEN POUNDS YA BIG FAT PUTZ
HOW TO TALK TO OTHER PEOPLE
BE A BETTER YOU ...OR ELSE
STOP PROCRASTINATING NOW!
FIX UP YOUR HOUSE
HOW TO BE GREAT IN BED
LEARN YOGA IN YOUR SLEEP

Never trust advice books.

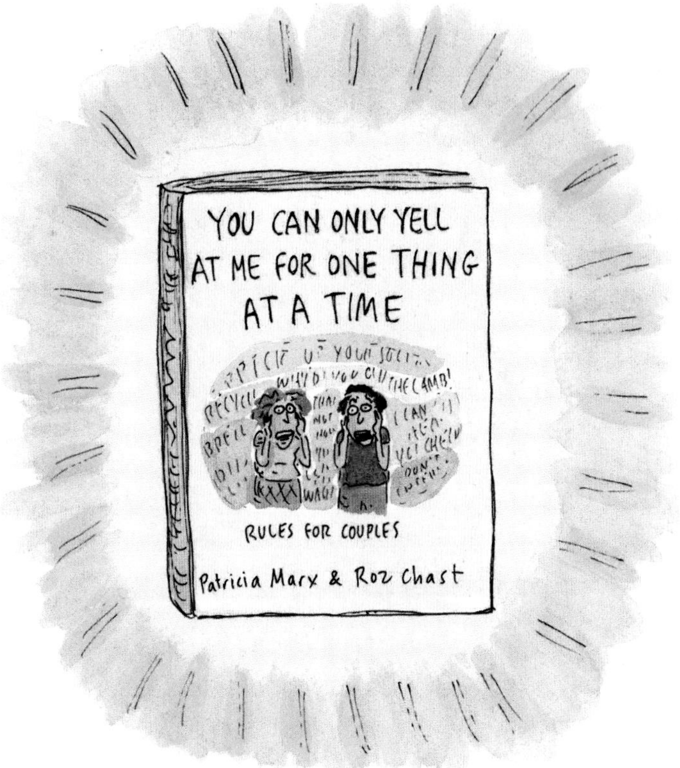
YOU CAN ONLY YELL AT ME FOR ONE THING AT A TIME
RULES FOR COUPLES
Patricia Marx & Roz Chast

Except this one.

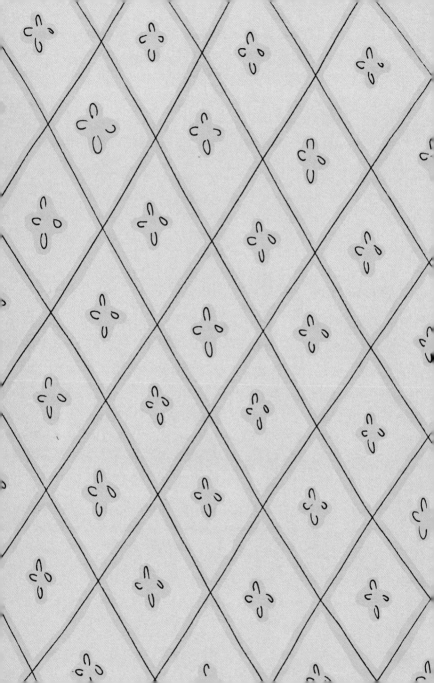

Acknowledgments

We are madly in love with our agents, Esther Newberg and Jin Auh, and our editor, Deb Futter. We also have unconditional love for everyone at Celadon, including Jamie Raab, Randi Kramer, Ryan Doherty, Cecily Van Buren-Freedman, Anne Twomey, Jonathan Bennett, Elizabeth Catalano, Karen Lumley, Christine Mykityshyn, Rachel Chou, Clay Smith, Anna Belle Hindenlang, Jaime Noven, Jennifer Jackson, Heather Orlando, Lauren Dooley, and Rebecca Ritchey.

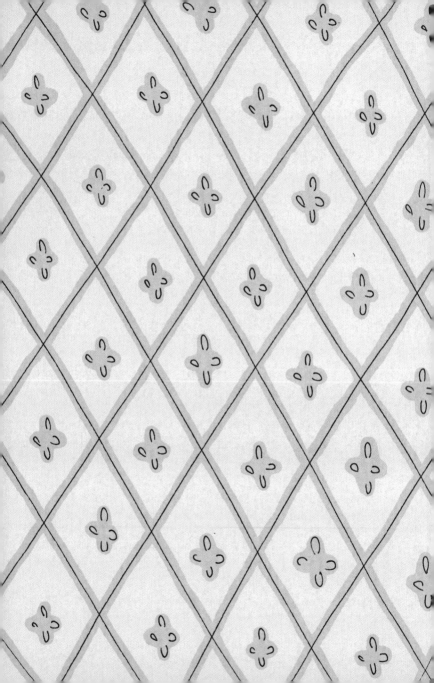

ABOUT THE AUTHOR

Patricia Marx has been contributing to *The New Yorker* since 1989. She is a former writer for *Saturday Night Live* and *Rugrats*, and is the author of several books, including *Let's Be Less Stupid*, *Him Her Him Again The End of Him*, and *Starting from Happy*. Marx was the first woman elected to the Harvard Lampoon. She has taught at Princeton, New York University, and Stonybrook University. She is a recipient of a Guggenheim Fellowship.

Photograph © Alexandra Penney

ABOUT THE ILLUSTRATOR

Roz Chast has loved to draw cartoons since she was a child growing up in Brooklyn. She attended Rhode Island School of Design, majoring in Painting because it seemed more artistic. However, soon after graduating, she reverted to type and began drawing cartoons once again. She is the author of the #1 *New York Times* bestselling memoir *Can't We Talk About Something More Pleasant?*

Photograph © Bill Franzen

CELADON
BOOKS
NEW YORK

Founded in 2017, Celadon Books, a division of
Macmillan Publishers, publishes a highly curated list
of twenty to twenty-five new titles a year. The list of
both fiction and nonfiction is eclectic and focuses
on publishing commercial and literary books and
discovering and nurturing talent.